# Table of Contents

Collected Writings On ... Exploring Biblical Faith .................................. 1

CHAPTER ONE: PRAYER AND FAITH (BOB ARMSTRONG) ................................................................. 3

CHAPTER TWO: FAITH AND MIRACLES (KEN RILEY) ....... 9

CHAPTER THREE: THE 'GALLERY OF FAITH' OF HEBREWS 11 (BRIAN FULLARTON) ................................ 14

CHAPTER FOUR: REPENTANCE AND FAITH (FRED EVANS) ........................................................................ 21

CHAPTER FIVE: FAITH IN ACTION - ABRAHAM (JOHN MILLER) ...................................................................... 25

CHAPTER SIX: FAITH IN ACTION - RAHAB (KEN RILEY) 29

CHAPTER SEVEN: FAITH THAT SAVES (FRED MCCORMICK) .............................................................. 34

CHAPTER EIGHT: PERSONAL FAITH (JOHN MILLER) ..... 43

CHAPTER NINE: FAITH IN ACTION – CALEB (ALAN TOMS) ........................................................................... 46

CHAPTER TEN: JUSTIFICATION BY FAITH AND BY WORKS (JACK FERGUSON) ........................................... 49

CHAPTER ELEVEN: THE SACRIFICE AND SERVICE OF FAITH (GUY JARVIE) ..................................................... 54

CHAPTER TWELVE: FAITH IN ACTION – TWO GENTILES (JOHN MILLER) ............................................................ 57

CHAPTER THIRTEEN: FAITH AND DOUBT (JACK GAULT)..................61

CHAPTER FOURTEEN: FAITH IN ACTION – MOSES (FRED EVANS)..................64

CHAPTER FIFTEEN: FAITH AND SPIRITUAL GROWTH (REG PARKER)..................69

CHAPTER SIXTEEN: FAITH IN ACTION – JACOB (ANON)..................73

CHAPTER SEVENTEEN: THE SHIELD OF FAITH (DAVID HYLAND)..................77

CHAPTER EIGHTEEN: FAITH AND UNBELIEF (JOHN TERRELL)..................79

CHAPTER NINETEEN: A QUESTION OF FAITH - IS YOUR GOD ABLE? (GUY JARVIE)..................84

CHAPTER TWENTY: DOUBTING THOMAS (KEN DRAIN)..................87

CHAPTER TWENTY-ONE: FAITH IN ACTION – THE WIDOW OF ZAREPHATH (REG DARKE)..................92

CHAPTER TWENTY-TWO: FAITH AND SCIENCE (LAURIE BURROWS)..................94

CHAPTER TWENTY-THREE: FAITH IN THE LIVING GOD (REG DARKE)..................100

CHAPTER TWENTY-FOUR: FAITH IN ACTION – EZEKIEL AND HIS WIFE (IAN LITHGOW)..................103

CHAPTER TWENTY-FIVE: "I BELIEVE GOD" (TOM HYLAND)..................106

CHAPTER TWENTY-SIX: FAITH IN ACTION – THE FIERY FURNACE (WILLIE STEWART) ........................................ 108

CHAPTER TWENTY-SEVEN: FAITH AND DIFFICULT QUESTIONS (PETER HICKLING) ................................................. 110

CHAPTER TWENTY-EIGHT: FAITH AND FEELINGS (ANON.) ........................................................................ 114

CHAPTER TWENTY-NINE: FAITH IN ACTION – ELIJAH (EDWIN STANLEY) ........................................................... 116

CHAPTER THIRTY: FAITH IN ACTION MISCELLANY (VARIOUS) ...................................................................... 119

CHAPTER THIRTY-ONE: YE OF LITTLE FAITH! (REG DARKE) ........................................................................ 128

# COLLECTED WRITINGS ON ...

# EXPLORING BIBLICAL FAITH

## HAYES PRESS

Copyright © Hayes Press 2016

All rights reserved. No part of this book may be reproduced, stored in a retrieval system, or transmitted in any form, without the written permission of Hayes Press.

Published by:

HAYES PRESS Publisher, Resources & Media,

The Barn, Flaxlands

Royal Wootton Bassett

Swindon, SN4 8DY

United Kingdom

[www.hayespress.org](http://www.hayespress.org)[1]

Unless otherwise indicated, all Scripture quotations are from the Revised Version Bible (1885, Public Domain). Scriptures marked NKJV are from the HOLY BIBLE, the New King James Version® (NKJV®). Copyright © 1982 Thomas Nelson, Inc. Used by permission. All rights reserved." Scriptures marked NIV are from New International Version®, NIV® Copyright © 1973, 1978, 1984, 2011 by Biblica, Inc.™ Used by permission. All rights reserved worldwide. Scriptures marked NASB are from the New American Standard

---

1. http://www.hayespress.org

Bible®, Copyright © 1960, 1962, 1963, 1968, 1971, 1972, 1973, 1975, 1977, 1995 by The Lockman Foundation. Used by permission." (www.Lockman.org)

**If you enjoy reading this book, we would really appreciate it if you could just take a couple of minutes to leave a brief review where you downloaded this book.**

# CHAPTER ONE: PRAYER AND FAITH (BOB ARMSTRONG)

"IF YE HAVE FAITH AS a grain of mustard seed, ye shall say unto this mountain, Remove hence to yonder place; and it shall remove; and nothing shall be impossible unto you" (Matt.17:20). The background of the Lord's amazing claim to faith's possibilities was the case of the epileptic boy (Matt.17:14-15): "There came to Him a man, kneeling to Him, and saying, Lord have mercy on my son: for he is epileptic, and suffereth grievously: for ofttimes he falleth into the fire, and oft-times into the water. And I brought him to Thy disciples, and they could not cure him."

There had been earlier and better days for the "disciples in training" with the Lord. It was perhaps a year earlier, in the Lord's Galilean ministry, when Luke 9:1-6 tells us: "He called the twelve together, and gave them power and authority over all demons, and to cure diseases ... and they departed, and went ... preaching the gospel, and healing everywhere".

Matthew 10 and Mark 6 record similar detail, putting it probably much earlier than the abortive attempt to exorcise the demon from the boy. They were glorious days, when they felt the pulse of divine power in their preaching as Satan's kingdom of darkness was shaken, and disease fled before the preaching of these anointed men. Written into the eternal record are the events of those momentous days. Communities were touched by the power of God, as disease-ridden people told how instant healing power gave them wholeness again. These events probably happened in the second and third journeys of the Lord in Galilee. The extent and magnitude of the Lord's healing ministry, shared by the disciples, was such that no other has ever effectively touched so many in so short a time. Someone has written, "He crowded into three short years actions and labours of love that might have adorned a century".

**Waning Power**

It may have been some twelve months later, and these same disciples were powerless to heal. According to the boy's father they had tried unsuccessfully to cast the tormenting demon from the boy's body. What had happened? Let's look at a number of possibilities.

1) Days without contact with the Lord.

2) Too busy to pray.

3) The success of their missions of healing may have gone to their heads in self-glory rather than God's glory.

4) Affected by the pride that goes before a fall.

Whatever is done in the Master's service, we must always remember that God has irrevocably declared, "I am the LORD; that is My Name and My glory will I not give to another" (Is.42:8). One of Satan's appealing devices is self-glory. God is under no obligation to bless those who are full of self and pride, which He hates. Whatever caused their failure, it produced the Lord's searching assessment, "O faithless and perverse generation, how long shall I be with you? How long shall I bear with you? Bring him hither to Me. And Jesus rebuked him and the demon went out from him: and the boy was. cured from that hour" (Matt.17:17,18).

As the disciples stood in the majestic light of their Master's presence, they must have felt like crawling into a corner to hide. Besides saying that the disciples were faithless He used another strong word "perverse". The Greek word means "distorted, misinterpreted, corrupted". He stated in strongest terms the character of their generation. Afterward, they asked the Lord an almost incredible question, "Why couldn't we drive it out?" Apparently they were totally unaware of their condition, and the barrier they had erected between themselves and the Lord. His answer was brief but penetrating: "Because of your little faith" (Matt.17:20). The KJV renders this word "unbelief", and there is a close affinity between unbelief and lack of faith. Their great Lord and Teacher had laid bare their spiritual anatomy as He diagnosed their spiritual condition. Good for us also to come under His kind but searching scrutiny.

**Fresh Challenge**

Looking again at the disciples' question, "Why couldn't we drive it out?", the Lord's answer, "Because of your little faith" was a sharp rebuke for their lack of confidence in Him, yet He did not abandon them. "The gifts and the calling of God are without repentance" (Rom.11:29). The Lord in His grace, gave them a fresh challenge by that historic statement, "if ye have faith as a grain of mustard seed, ye shall say unto this mountain, Remove hence to yonder place; and it shall remove; and nothing shall be impossible to you". In the days of the disciples' subsequent reflection, they probably wondered why the same words they had used many times before had failed to expel the demon from the boy.

How often in our own experience the word has been preached and the power of the Holy Spirit through God's message has led people to the Saviour. At other times the same word has been preached, with seemingly negative response. Can we ever leave the scene of fruitless service without some soul-searching? External forces are at work and Satan "blinds the minds of them that believe not". Internally, lack of faith, unbelief, pride, unconfessed sin, will hinder the work of the Holy Spirit. Personal holiness and moral purity are essential in those who would serve the Lord in witnessing. Matthew 13:54-58 shows that unbelief in the hearer can also hinder the Spirit's work. "He did not many mighty works there because of their unbelief". However, we must not overlook what appears as a sovereign law of God in Isaiah 55:11, "So shall My word be that goeth forth out of My mouth: it shall not return unto Me void, but it shall accomplish that which I please, and it shall prosper in the thing whereto I sent it".

**Moving Mountains**

If all the conditions in Matthew 17:20 were met, the Lord said a mountain could be moved, and He reinforced the supernatural by saying to the disciples, "and nothing shall be impossible to you". The Lord Jesus was simply teaching, that in response to the kind of faith He defined, there was no question but that the creative energies and power of God could lift that mountain right off its foundation and set it down elsewhere. All those forces and powers are resident in the Godhead. The Lord wanted the disciples to learn that. He wants us to learn it too. He did not tell them to do it, but only to believe He could do it. "All things were made by Him; and without Him was not anything made that hath been made" wrote John years later.

That brings us to Hebrews 11:1: "faith is the assurance of things hoped for, the proving of things not seen". Faith is real when it does not see the event promised or performed, but patiently waits for it. "Hope that is seen is not hope" (Rom.8:24). The Lord did not intend that the disciples should forthwith go around moving mountains to prove their rejuvenated faith, but rather that they believe His word. The Lord was teaching them lessons in faith for the days long after the miraculous age. Years of suffering and persecution lay ahead for these men when it would be safer to say "Caesar is lord" than "Christ is Lord"; days when the deep roots of faith rather than miracles would sustain them in the enveloping darkness of a pagan world.

## Prayer and Faith

Prayer is the longing of the heart poured out. Faith is the assurance of the thing longed for. Our Lord encouraged His disciples "always to pray, and not to faint" (Lk.18:1). Then He told the story of the judge who said "no" to the widow who made him say "yes". By her persistent coming with the same request for justice, she wore him down until he handed down a verdict in her favour, to get the case off the books. Three lessons emerge.

1) Faith - the woman believed she would be avenged of her adversary. Had not the Lord told His disciples, "All things whatsoever ye pray and ask for believe that ye have received them, and ye shall have them" (Mk.11:24). Praying in the Holy Spirit is believing prayer, for "He maketh intercession for the saints according to the will of God" (Rom.8:27).

2) Fervency - the widow was fervent in her request, born of the urgency of her case, perhaps a life and death situation. Fervency in prayer is often lacking. Fervent prayers are effective prayers. "Elijah was a man of like passions with us, and he prayed fervently that it might not rain; and it rained not on the earth for three years and six months. And he prayed again: and the heaven gave rain" (Jas.5:17-18). In the shadows of Gethsemane our beloved Lord, "being in an agony, prayed more earnestly".

3) Perseverance - the woman persevered and gave no rest to the callous indifferent judge, until the answer came. We do not always receive immediate answers to prayer, but we must persevere as long as we are assured it is in the will of God. "With all prayer and supplication praying at all seasons in the Spirit, and watching thereunto in all perseverance and supplication for all the saints" (Eph.6:18). May the

Lord the Spirit take us past time-worn cliches in prayer, and the deadness some prayer meetings project. May we learn to pray the prayer of God the Holy Spirit through us.

"In nothing be anxious; but in everything by prayer and supplication with thanksgiving let your requests be made known unto God. And the peace of God which passeth all understanding, shall guard your hearts and your thoughts in Christ Jesus" (Phil.4:6,7). At this desperate moment of history, so near to the Lord's return, God has promised that this model for prayer will quieten the turmoil of anxiety and stress, flooding the mind and heart with a peace that transcends all understanding. Someone has written:

"There's no weapon half so mighty as the intercessors bear,

Nor a broader field of service than the ministry of prayer"

# CHAPTER TWO: FAITH AND MIRACLES (KEN RILEY)

A VITAL ELEMENT IN all the miracles of Jesus is the exercise of faith. But faith is a fragile plant that requires nurturing which the disciples recognized when they said "Lord, increase our faith". We are going to consider the exercise of faith evidenced in four miracles; how that faith grew and how it was rewarded.

John 4:46-54 records a miracle that took place in Cana where the Lord had turned the water into wine. We are introduced to a nobleman (or royal official) whose home was at Capernaum, about 20 miles distant. This man had faith enough to make the journey to Cana but not sufficient faith at first to believe that the Lord could heal at a distance. In this his faith was weaker than that of the centurion (Matt.8:8). That man's faith was great enough to say that if he, as a simple soldier, could expect his troops to do as he commanded, then the All-Powerful Lord could also give commands and they would be obeyed no matter how far the command had to travel, perhaps relying on the Scripture: "He sendeth His word, and healeth them" (Ps.107:20).

In the case before us, the Lord tested the faith of the nobleman whose response was still a plea to come down before his son died. There was still a lack of faith in being unable to believe that the Lord could raise from the dead, a lack that was to be found among even closer disciples. But his faith was growing, and hearing the word of the Lord that his son lived, he returned home. What authority there was in the Lord's voice that the man began the homeward journey, assured that there must have been an improvement in the boy's condition. It was not until the next day that he asked his servants when the cure had begun, only to be told that at the precise hour when the Lord actually spoke the words the fever had immediately left the boy. Little wonder at the effect it had, that his whole household, wife, children and servants should believe on the Lord and the potency of His word that, travelling faster even than light, could effect an immediate cure.

The demoniac child in Mark 9:14-29 was a sad case indeed. The father confessed that the boy was his only child - the male which had opened the womb. What sadness to realize that this is the one who should have been holy unto the Lord (Lk.2:23), but who had been taken over by the evil one to be the body in which his minion should dwell.

In the Lord's absence on the Mount of Transfiguration the father had brought the child to the remaining disciples who had earlier experienced demons being in subjection to them (Mk.6:13), but now are confronted with a case that was beyond their powers. Where was the lack of faith this time? There was a real lack of faith on the part of the father, and the faith of the disciples was not as great as it could have been if they had spent more time in prayer, having assessed that, in the inverted hierarchy of hell, there are some spirits more evil than others. There was certainly a lack of faith on the part of the scribes who were only too anxious to point out that impotence on the part of the disciples argued an impotence on the part of their Master.

Is there also an indication of lack of faith on the part of those in the neighbourhood when we read of the healing of the blind man who, at the first, could only see men as trees walking (Mk.8:22-26)? That miracle was worked in Bethsaida, of which the Lord had said that if the mighty works done there had been done in Tyre and Sidon the latter would have repented long ago (Matt.11:21). Again in Matthew 13:58 it is said "He did not do many miracles there because of their jack of faith" (NIV). In this case both the father and the crowds needed a vast increase in their faith. The father's words "If Thou canst" show how far he was away from true belief in the power of the Lord. It was these words that the Lord rebuked and caused the father to say "I do believe, help me overcome my unbelief" (NIV). What a cry from the heart of a needy man, and how it should be echoed in the hearts of all who are searching for salvation and a deepening of spiritual life. Our feeble faith can only reach so far, but "the Lord's hand is not shortened that it cannot save" (Is.59:1).

Our third miracle, in Matthew 9:27-31, is one of the many healings of the blind that took place when the Lord was on earth. Travellers in the East know of the greater prevalence of blindness there compared with more temperate countries. The sand of the desert and the dust of the ground are doubtless the cause of much blindness in these lands and the Lord knew what suffering was experienced not only by the blind person but by their immediate families. In many such cases we read that the Lord touched the eyes of the person, sometimes with saliva, sometimes with clay and sometimes healing by touch alone. Here again a measure of faith was exhibited by the blind men and it grew until they obtained what they desired. They cried out in the first place, "Have mercy on us, Thou son of David".

In this they recognized His claims as the Messiah, but only the Lord could know if the words came from sincere hearts or from flattering lips. He tested their faith by continuing on His journey, an action that necessitated the blind men following Him, despite their difficulty in keeping up, until they came to the house where the Lord was. These had been no words of flattery but a genuine desire to receive their sight from the only Man who could give it them. It was then that He touched their eyes, saying, "According to your faith be it done unto you", and at the word their eyes were opened. As one has said, "Faith is the bucket of heavenly grace and of our salvation, by which we drink from the well which we can reach by no other means".

Our last miracle is that of the paralytic man in Luke 5:17-26 borne by four of his friends. The setting of this miracle is in the presence of the Pharisees and doctors of the law who had come not only from every village in Galilee but also from Jerusalem, the seat of learning. Let us hope that the object of their coming together was in a genuine spirit of wanting to learn more of this Teacher that had arisen in Israel and who was doing such mighty works among them. What hope had four friends of bringing a needy paralytic to the Lord when the path to the door was so crowded? But a faith that will climb knows no barriers; the way to the roof was open, and the roof itself was soon going to be opened as well. It would appear that the Lord was discoursing in the upper room of the house when the roof was uncovered and the paralytic let down.

It is here that some have limited the faith to the four bearers, but who can limit faith to these faithful four? Did not the fifth man have as great a faith as his friends? What extra suffering he must have endured as he was carried up to the roof. Could he not have cried out "Why trouble the Master any further?" What embarrassment he must have suffered when the eyes of the great men of Israel looked upon him with disdain, annoyed as they already would have been at the dust of the roof falling upon them. No, his faith was as great as the bearers and the Lord looked upon him with the words, "Man, thy sins are forgiven thee".

The Lord knew the man's first need. The man himself knew that he was a sinner. Perhaps he was suffering pain because of some special sin, and needed the peace in his heart that the Lord's words alone could bring. It brought an uncalled-for response on the part of the lawyers who knew that only God could forgive sins. It was easy to say words like that because no one on earth could prove whether the sins were forgiven or not. But easy as the words were to say, the work of salvation at Calvary was a task beyond the ability of any other to accomplish. The Lord's following words proved not only could He heal, but that He had power on earth to forgive sins. The man was raised up and walked away, carrying the mat that had so recently carried him; he doubtless found that the path to the door was so much easier than the approach that he and his friends had tried to make earlier. All were now anxious to make way for the one of whose healing they could say, "We have seen strange things today".

Little wonder that the disciples could say to the Lord, "Increase our faith". We, too, cry out with the father of the boy, "I do believe, help me overcome my unbelief."

# CHAPTER THREE: THE 'GALLERY OF FAITH' OF HEBREWS 11 (BRIAN FULLARTON)

**FAITH - NECESSITY**

Jesus, in saying to the disciples "Blessed are the eyes which see the things that ye see", was not referring to physical objects perceived by natural sight but to what was the subject of divine revelation; spiritual truths seen by the eye of faith. As natural sight is precious so is faith's vision of the realm of the spiritual. When this vision dims, the life of faith will suffer. The sublime operations of the ways and works of God are spiritually discerned (1 Cor.2:14). Most often 'believing' is 'seeing', not vice versa. The spiritual landscape brought into view by the focus of the eye of faith is rich and breathtaking. A believer's progress is not maintained with reference to the visible landmarks of this passing world. Faith guarantees perseverance. Without faith, ever present and sinister forces pitted against the Christian would prove too powerful.

It is not easy to fulfil the exhortation "Walk by faith" (2 Cor.5:7) in a hostile, material world, largely atheistic and scornful of faith. Yet all has been foreseen by a merciful God who has "granted unto us all things that pertain unto life and godliness" (2 Pet.1:3). Men and women of faith are sustained and spurred on by looking to Jesus, the Pioneer and Perfecter of faith.

**The Wider Context**

Repeatedly in this epistle the importance of faith is emphasized as being the principle which should govern a life well-pleasing to God. Attention has been drawn in the preceding chapters to the perils of unbelief. Spiritual disaster will result from the abandonment of faith. By the command of God the visible creation was brought into existence; it can be accounted for in no other way. Scientific research deals with what exists; the question of discovery of ultimate origin must be the quest of faith. The inspired writer regards faith as spiritual apprehension of divine truth. It produces inward conviction and certainty of the reality of the unseen, does not seek full explanations but accepts unquestionably the revelation of God. Eternal things become factual and real.

Quotation has already been made of Habakkuk's profound statement, "My righteous one shall live by faith" (Heb.10:38). In the first six verses of chapter 11 the writer now describes vividly the effects of faith, and this description is followed by a series of wonderfully depicted profiles of outstanding personalities of Bible history, whose lives were marked by this virtue. The heroes of faith are not chosen at random. They are carefully selected as appropriate to the main theme of the epistle, namely the supremacy and excellence of Christ over all others; selected also to encourage the saints of these early days to avert the danger of deserting their new Leader and reverting to their old life.

The men and women of Hebrews 11 acted and lived in the light of revelation from God which altered the course of their lives. They perceived by faith the unseen and eternal. Seven men and one woman of faith are mentioned by name in the period from the beginning of God's work with the human race until the Law (vv.4-23). The same number are connected with the kingdom and nation of Israel (vv.23-32). In all these individuals faith was tested under the most severe conditions. Faith was the salient feature and nothing seemed impossible where it existed.

**From Abel to Abraham (vv.1-12)**

Remarkable light is thrown upon the faith of many, faith which is sometimes not readily observed from the record in Genesis and Exodus. God alone sees faith where men often attribute failure. In some lives, of course, failure gives place to faith.

In Abel, the first martyr, faith led to sacrifice spiritually then physically. Accepted by God, he was hated by his brother. Today, Cain's error is repeated in the attachment of men to their works, seeking justification before God. In rejecting the way to God through the virtue of Christ's offering of Himself they stain their hands with blood exceedingly more precious than Abel's (cf. Heb.10:29). Faith is the initial and continual condition of approach to God. Testimony was borne by God to Abel's faith. That faith is still speaking today.

Enoch's faith led to fellowship, walking with God in the midst of increasing perversity (Jude 14,15). He suffered mocking and reproach. The occasion would come later when there would be the visible token of God's presence and dwelling with men in the cloud of glory. The absence of this gave more opportunity for the fuller exercise of faith in acknowledging the reality of God's Person and Presence.

Noah is next cited. His life of faith produced witness, for in action and word he was a preacher of righteousness. His godly fear and devout life, emphasized by references in Ezekiel (14:14) and Peter (2 Pet.2:5) enabled him with patient endurance to live by faith. The consideration of Him who patiently endured the gainsaying of sinners in His pathway will prevent fainting in our souls and waxing weary in the road of conflict (12:3).

Abraham trusted God, believed His promise and obeyed His word. He was willing to live as an alien in the country given to him in promise and viewed his accommodation as temporary. As through a telescope, his faith could see the eternal city planned and prepared by God in reward to faith. His faith and implicit obedience had a profound effect upon his progeny. Sarah, his wife, turned from disbelief to faith. Laughter at the idea of conceiving a son in advanced years betrayed scepticism and brought rebuke from the Lord. Faith finally soared above doubt in acceptance of God's promise.

**Strangers and Pilgrims (vv. 13-16)**

The lovely epitome of these verses shows stamina being produced by faith when it is accompanied by witness - "they that say such things" (v.14). In faith they lived, in faith they died. The call of God was heard and obeyed. Eagerly they sought the fulfilment of the promises, having greeted them, yet they did not receive them in the fuller sense (v.40). As pilgrims in this world they started on the long trek of faith, distant prospects appearing just over the horizon, courageous travellers longing for their permanent home. Their native soil held no attraction for them; they could have returned had they so desired. Their ambitions and aspirations were independent of this age, scavengers of this world's paltry fare they would not be. They moved out in faith's expedition, "wherefore God is not ashamed of them, to be called their God" (v.16).

**From Abraham to Joshua (vv. 17-31)**

The writer resumes the story of Abraham in relating the event of Genesis 22 and draws out faith's triumph when tried. Isaac's death would nullify God's promises of the Seed, the land and the nation but Abraham's faith was equal to the test. He knew the truth of resurrection and acted through faith in believing God would raise his son from the dead. This typified the work of God at a later date in full accomplishment through the death and resurrection of the Only-begotten from the Father.

Isaac by faith blessed Jacob and Esau. From the Genesis record a very different conclusion could be drawn by the casual observer. The younger son deceived his father. Isaac had preferred the first-born, Esau, but realized that the purposes of God must stand (Gen.25:23), and so did not cancel the blessing given to Jacob (27:33). Esau was given a subsidiary blessing (27:39,40). Notice is made of Jacob's bright faith at the end of a tumultuous and sometimes dangerous career, not the disturbing episodes of his varied experiences. With clear perspective he saw the meaning of the past and the future in the prophetic benediction upon Joseph's two boys. The brief reference to Joseph highlights the sovereign divine insight which selected his dying request as evidence of his faith. Where men might have expected the historical landmarks of his trials, humiliation, exaltation and magnificence, the inspired commentator speaks of Joseph's faith in the exodus of his people and the disposal of Joseph's bones. Egypt had no place in Joseph's heart. He desired no permanent epigraph of his stay there, no elaborate funeral, no ostentatious sepulchre or Egyptian pyramid. The land of promise would be the place of awakening on the resurrection morning.

Moses refused, chose, accounted, looked, forsook and endured. These are activities of faith to be pondered. God saw in his heart a deep-settled faith. Moses renounced earthly advantages and bound up his life with the people of God, choosing the reproach of Christ in suffering affliction rather than the sampling of fleeting pleasures. Comforts of a palace existence were shunned and deemed as dross. The status of being the son of Pharaoh's daughter held no appeal. Ill-treatment there was in the way of faith but greater riches and joys awaited him. Forsaking and enduring are the outcome of faith.

No mention is made of faith during Israel's wilderness wanderings. Failure characterized them. Refreshing it is to see the faith of the nation being the key to victory in the book of Joshua (v.30). The Red Sea crossing and capture of Jericho were examples of faith in God's word and promise. Rahab's background declares eloquently God's dealings in grace universally. She placed in Israel's God the faith which comes of hearing, repudiated nationalistic feelings and a profligate life to find a place among the people of God and in the genealogy of Jesus Christ (Matt.1).

**Judges, Kings and Prophets (vv. 32-40)**

Any secular historian would have devoted more space to the names and events of these verses. The hearers and readers of this letter must have been profoundly touched when being reminded of these exploits of faith. The pathos deepens with the pace of the narrative. Reflecting upon these monuments to faith, all of whom clearly and firmly grasped the invisible and unseen, there is challenge. They stand as a line of witnesses against the inclination to unbelief.

The deeds and trials of faith enumerated in vv. 33-38 are not exclusive to certain known figures of the sacred record. The unending line of faithful witnesses had divested themselves of all impediments and every weight of the pressures and anxieties of this life and the sin of unbelief. Prospectively, they looked unto Christ - their Leader and Chief. He sustained them. They say to us what the life of faith meant to them. The life of faith was a quest of love and humility, not a grudging duty. There was determination to share the glorious vision with others. The world is not worthy of such, but the coming world is! The present world is nonetheless the arena of conflict and the sphere for faith's work.

**Christ Above All**

'These all' (v.39) had witness borne to them by God and His word. Only the divine revelation of faith's Originator, the Son of God, could secure the better thing and provide the long-awaited realization of God's purpose. Faults and failures there were in their lives but these are omitted in line with the promise of the previous chapter, "their sins and their iniquities will I remember no more" (10:17). The Lord Jesus had no lapses from beginning to end of His life of faith. His circumstances were considerably more difficult. He won the highest honours by the way of faith through death to the goal of heavenly glory. Supreme He stands, not only over all creation, in redemption and resurrection but also in faith.

# CHAPTER FOUR: REPENTANCE AND FAITH (FRED EVANS)

IN HIS FAREWELL ADDRESS to the overseers of the Ephesian assembly, Paul the apostle claimed that he had not shrunk from "testifying both to Jews and to Greeks repentance toward God, and faith toward our Lord Jesus Christ" (Acts 20:21). The two truths are linked together. Paul preached repentance as a command from God. Man's course by nature had proved to be leading downwards - away from God. The creature had moved away from his Creator on a track contrary to His desire. In nature and results the controversy had always been the same. Even when the Son of God was manifested on earth, under these decidedly changed conditions the result was still the same - downwards and away from God. Thus Paul preached "repentance toward God" - turning towards God and looking towards Him.

**Linked Together**

With the appearance of Jesus Christ on earth, both repentance and faith were brought into sharp focus. They are not essentially successive stages in conversion, and it would seem to be unwise to consider them chronologically as to which comes first. In the presence of a rejected Christ, the controversy between God and man now centred in Him. All would need to acknowledge their need of Christ, believing in Him, and turning to God through Him. To place faith in Christ would involve a turning of the heart to Him, as the only true way to God. There is no coming to God but in the strength of Jesus Christ as Mediator. It is the goodness of God that leads to repentance and opens the door of faith (Rom.2:4).

**Repentance**

The New Testament word for repentance signifies a change of mind, so leading to a change of conduct. To repent is "to think differently or afterwards, to reconsider". This afterthought obviously implies a reversal of an earlier decision or line of conduct, from bad to good. There is a turning of the heart from sin to God. The person has a conviction of the evil consequence of sin, a conviction produced in the mind by the Holy Spirit. The result is godly sorrow, accompanied by faith in Christ. This change of mind is not merely an intellectual one but a change of the man himself, the real man. It is not comparable with the Roman Catholic penitence or penance, but is the turning of the mind or heart to God. As Paul says, "I myself with the mind serve the law of God" (Rom.7.25).

Let us take an example. When Paul stood before the influential court of judges on Mars Hill, he made it very clear that God was now commanding all men everywhere to repent (Acts 17:22-34). Among the Athenians idolatry was rampant. Objects of worship were numerous gold, silver, stone, "graven by art and device of man". So Paul sought earnestly to lead them to the knowledge of the true and living God, that they might worship Him. He cogently set Him forth as the great Creator of heaven and earth and of all men. The eternal Giver, the omnipotent God, provides for all, life and breath and all things. Of one man He had made every nation on all the face of the earth, having predetermined their appointed seasons and the bounds of their habitats. In Him all men live, and move, and have their being. Every one of the human race is within easy reach of Him, and if they only felt after Him they would find Him.

How absurd of the Athenians to be worshipping other gods – man-made idols and images, and even an unknown god! They needed to repent of their idolatry - it was sheer ignorance on their part. It was obviously necessary for them to turn to the living and true God. He Himself was commanding them to do so, to change their minds and their ways, to turn with sorrow and shame from sin, and with cheerfulness and resolution to every Christian duty. Especially so, as God Himself had provided a Saviour in the person of His only begotten Son whom He had raised from the dead and ordained to be the Judge of all the world.

Did any of the people of Athens repent? Happily, yes. Certain of them repented and believed. Dionysius, a learned judge at the court, was converted and entered into fellowship with Paul and other disciples. There is some reason to surmise that he was eventually burnt to death as a Christian martyr in Athens itself. Another convert was "a woman named Damaris", of whom very little is known. And there were others with them. These are splendid illustrations of repentant ones as denoted in Paul's address to king Agrippa, when he attested that he had declared to Jews and Gentiles "that they should repent and turn to God, doing works worthy of repentance" (Acts 26:20).

**Faith**

Faith in Christ is especially reliance upon Him for salvation. It comes by hearing, and hearing by the word of Christ (Rom.10:17). Not by persuasive words of man's wisdom, nor by clever reasoning founded on basic facts. The sinner hears the voice of God, he believes in Christ, and he is accounted righteous in God's sight. He is born again, of the Spirit. The record God has given of His Son has been accepted, the testimony to Christ, and he has placed his faith in Him personally. This gives assurance and conviction.

It is a mistake to look on our faith as the little we must do to make up the price of our redemption. There is only one Redeemer, and He has paid the whole price. The ransomed sinner has heard the voice of the Redeemer, and on hearing the gospel message he has placed his trust in the living Christ of God. His faith at first laid hold on the message and "by it he gained an eternal standing-ground upon the Rock of Ages". He believes with his heart (Rom.10:9) and the free gift of God is his - eternal life.

"Faith is the assurance of things hoped for". In things we hope for it gives a sure confidence. There is a spiritual conviction, a trustworthy expectation that God will perform all that He has promised to us in Christ.

"Faith is ... the proving of things not seen". For things we do not see, it provides certainty and proof. "It demonstrates to the eye of the mind the reality of those things that cannot be discerned by the eye of the body". It reveals as real fact what is not revealed to the senses. The believer is served by faith instead of sight (Heb.11:1).

## Conclusion

During His life on earth the Saviour recognized faith in those who appealed to Him for help. He looked for a response to Himself, a readiness to accept what He had to give. After the crucifixion and resurrection, faith in the sense of utter trust in Jesus for salvation became richer in content and stronger in grasp. The Saviour still looks for this response in sinners coming to Him, as they turn towards Him in faith. Not only at the time of conversion but throughout the whole Christian life. "We through the Spirit by faith wait for the hope of righteousness ... faith working through love" (Gal.5:5,6). Faith becomes operative through love: this is the all-important link between faith in Christ and love in Christian character.

# CHAPTER FIVE: FAITH IN ACTION - ABRAHAM (JOHN MILLER)

WHILST THERE WERE MEN of faith before the time of Abraham, and three of these are specifically mentioned in Hebrews 11, Abel, Enoch, and Noah, yet it is to Abraham that Paul goes back when he deals with the important matter of justification by faith in the epistles to the Romans and the Galatians. Abraham was a man of faith before he left Ur of the Chaldees.

When the God of glory appeared to him in Ur He told him to leave the land of his birth and to come into a land that He would show him He went out by faith, not knowing where he was going. The call of God went deeper than that of leaving one land and going to another. It involved his leaving his kindred and his father's house. These conditions of separation were completed when he left Haran and entered the land of Canaan as we read in Genesis 12. Though Lot his nephew went with him the time came when the cleavage took place between Lot and his uncle, when Lot chose the pleasant land of the Jordan valley, where the cities of Sodom and Gomorrah were, and he descended to that land of fruitfulness but moral degradation.

War broke out in the land of Lot's choice, and he and his family and his goods were carried away with the goods and captives from the cities of the plain. When Abraham heard of Lot being carried away, he hastily set out in pursuit of the invading and victorious armies with the object of delivering Lot. In a night attack upon those armies near to the city of Damascus, Abraham smote and pursued them to Hobah. He brought back all the goods, also Lot and his goods, and the women and the people. These things we find in Genesis 14.

Then in Genesis 15 we are told that the Lot appeared to Abraham in a vision, and said to him, "Fear not, Abram: I am thy shield, and thy exceeding great reward" (verse 1). It may well be that Abram's thoughts were seriously disturbed as he thought of what might be the consequences of his attacking the armies of four great powers in the world at that time. Would they return and pour out their vengeance upon him? And what could he do to withstand them with the few men he had? The Lord assured Abram that He was his shield, and what blows there might be from the enemy, they would not fall upon him.

Abram did not discuss the matter of his protection but he laid hold on the matter of reward; so he asked, "O Lord GOD, what wilt Thou give me, seeing I go childless, and he that shall be possessor of my house is Dammesek Eliezer (Eliezer of Damascus)? And Abram said, Behold, to me Thou hast given no seed: and, lo, one born in my house is mine heir." The promise made to Abram when the Lord called him in Ur was that God would make of him a great nation (Gen.12:2), yet Sarah his wife had no children. Could God's promise fail? God's promises do not fail; the failure may lie with us through our lack of faith. Sarah, Abram's wife, gave her handmaid to Abram, as recorded in the next chapter (Gen.16), in the hope that she might obtain children by her handmaid, but that was not God's way.

God assured Abram that Eliezer would not be his heir, but one born of himself would be his heir. He brought Abram out and it was night, and the heavens were beautiful as lighted by the infinite number of stars, and he was told to tell, that is to number, the stars, and the LORD said, "So shall thy seed be." What could Abram do? He could not number the stars. No one can, even in this day with the numerous instruments men possess. What did he do? "He believed in the LORD; and He counted it to him for righteousness." It was night and everything was dark on earth, but the heavens were bright with light, and brighter than they was the promise contained in God's word. "So shall thy seed be."

Whoever had a hand in arranging the inspired books of the New Testament, and placing the epistle to the Romans at the beginning of the epistles, had a clear insight into the character of the teaching of this epistle. It is the great gospel episode, and shows clearly how the sinner who believes in Christ is justified by faith. It was written to the saints in the church of God in Rome. Though it was written to the saints in Rome, yet the present church of Rome denies that the believer in Christ is justified by faith, despite the words of Romans 5.1 (KJV): "Therefore being justified by faith, we have peace with God through our Lord Jesus Christ." Rome teaches that the sinner is justified by his own works and sufferings: the gospel teaches that we are justified by faith in the work of Christ on the Cross. There He bore the sins of the sinner in His body on the tree (1 Pet.2:24). This was written by the man that Rome teaches was the first pope. Peter also said. "To Him bear all the prophets witness, that through His name every one that believeth on Him shall receive remission of sins" (Acts 10:43). When the believer's sins are forgiven, he is justified by faith.

These two truths are joined by Paul in Romans 4.2-5: "If Abraham was justified by works, he hath whereof to glory; but not toward God. For what saith the scripture? And Abraham believed God, and it was reckoned unto him for righteousness. Now to him that worketh, the reward is not reckoned as of grace, but as of debt. But to him that worketh not, but believeth on Him that justifieth the ungodly, has faith is reckoned for righteousness."

Words could not make the matter of justification by faith clearer. The one whose sins are forgiven by believing is the same one who is justified by faith. In Romans 4:25 we have the matter of the death and resurrection joined, "Who [Jesus our Lord] was delivered up for our trespasses, and was raised for our justification".

(1) "It is God that justifieth" (Rom.8:33). God is the justifier of the one who is justified by faith. Faith excludes the believer's works. God challenges anyone in regard to His act of justification with the words, "Who is he 'that shall condemn?" He has a strong neck and a hard heart who would challenge the work of God.

(2) "Being justified freely by His grace" (Rom.3:24). God justifies freely by His grace. Grace shuts out all human merit, the merit of human works or any other kind of merit. This statement of God's grace in justification comes in after the statement of Romans 3:23, "For all have sinned, and fall short of the glory of God." The whole world is brought under the judgement of God (Rom.3:19). There is not one man of this world that doeth good and sinneth not. God could find no other way of dealing with men than in grace.

(3) "Being now justified by His blood" (Rom.5.9). "Being now justified by His blood, shall we be saved from the wrath of God through Him." "His blood" not only shows how it is possible for God to be just and yet justify the believing sinner, but also tells the infinite cost of a sinner being justified. There would have been no possible justification for man apart from the blood, that is, the death of the Lord.

(4) "Being therefore justified by faith" (Rom.5:1). Then as to the justifying of a sinner, this is the condition that God lays down, that the sinner must believe in the Lord Jesus Christ. An easier and more simple condition could not be conceived. On the ground of faith and that alone will a sinner be justified, and be at peace with God.

# CHAPTER SIX: FAITH IN ACTION - RAHAB (KEN RILEY)

THE MIND OF JOSHUA must have gone back forty years when he looked over the Jordan to the Promised Land. He had then been a young man and had gone to spy out the land on behalf of the people. They had wanted a report on that land despite the fact that God had promised it to them and they should have gone in by faith. Moses had agreed to their request and God had given His approval, for He knew the weaknesses in the heart of man (cf. Deut.1:22,23 with Num.13:2). What a tragedy that spying expedition had turned out to be. Only he and Caleb had come back with a recommendation to go in and possess the land, but the people had rebelled and he had had to wait for forty years before the land had come into view again.

It was now he and not Moses who had to decide the next step. This time there was to be no public choosing of spies to bring back a report on the land. This time the spies were to be chosen secretly and sent in order to seek out the weak spots in the land's defences so that Joshua could work out his military strategy. The two spies were hand-picked men who were being sent out on a particularly dangerous mission and they were well aware that no mercy would be shown to them were they to fall into the hands of the people of Jericho.

It was of God's overruling that they found their way to Rahab's house. Foreign travellers would be marked men in a city which knew of the presence of a large army on the other side of Jordan. But entry into the house of a harlot caused no raising of eyebrows in lascivious Jericho and the spies could have found no safer refuge. That Rahab was a harlot and not just an innkeeper (as stated by Josephus and the Rabbis) is beyond doubt. The Hebrew word allows of no other translation and the description of Rahab in the New Testament leaves no cause for misunderstanding.

The spies arrived in Jericho at dusk and could have been in Rahab's house for no more than two hours before the king's men arrived. In that short time Rahab had been convinced that it was God's intention to destroy Jericho and that no matter how broad the wall and how strong the defences, Jericho was doomed. Hebrews 11:31 tells us that she perished not with the disobedient. All in Jericho had the same evidence as Rahab had even before the spies arrived. But whilst the rest of the city were disobedient only one was found whose faith transcended the walls of the city and rested in Jehovah, the God of Israel. Truly, "the tax collectors and the prostitutes are entering the kingdom of God ahead of you" (Matt.21:31).

By faith, Rahab hid the spies. That faith had been in existence, albeit feeble, before the spies came, and was strengthened by their witness. Her hiding of the two men and the sending of the hunt on a wild goose chase could be construed as an act of treason which it undoubtedly was in the eyes of men. But in the eyes of God her action was one of faith. Her telling of lies to the hunters cannot be justified. She had yet to learn that God does not need the lying testimony of men for the working out of His purposes and we cannot expect of a newly born convert the deep knowledge of God's will that an older disciple should have. Although adultery and lying are never condoned by God, "Thou shalt not commit adultery" and "Thou shalt not bear false witness" were specific commands to a people of God who were going to be given the presence of the Almighty God to give them the strength to obey. Rahab was still on the learning curve as were the inhabitants of a latter day Jericho to whom Paul could write "And that is what some of you were: But you were washed, you were sanctified, you were justified in the name of the Lord Jesus Christ" (1 Cor.6:11).

In response to the actions of Rahab, the men promised that they would protect her when Israel took the city. Doubtless they thought that there would be a frontal attack on the weakest part of Jericho and that hand-to-hand fighting would take place in the streets. Rahab's house was on the wall, possibly near the town's gates and therefore at the strongest point. No frontal attack would be made there and they would do their best to see that Rahab's house was protected from the fiercest fighting. God honoured their promise which had been made without His prior consent. He had said that all the cities were to be "devoted" (see Deut.20:16-18 JWM), but He honoured this pledge even as He was going to honour a pledge given to the Gibeonites without His being previously consulted. The promise, however, was a limited one. Only those who were in the house would be safe. Any that took their chance in the street would forfeit all right to protection. And the sign of the scarlet cord would be there to enable the Israelites to honour their obligation. Did the spies remember that it was the scarlet blood on the doorposts and lintels of their fathers' houses that had saved them? To the inhabitants of Jericho it was no more than the sign they would expect in the window of such a woman, but to the armies outside it was the sign of the house that was to be protected at all costs even though the protector might lose his own life in the process.

It was here that the faith of Rahab was communicated to others. When the city was surrounded she persuaded all her family to squeeze into her small house. Some of them may have said, "why go to the wall? That is the spot that is nearest to the invading army. Surely the safest place is in the centre of the city furthest away from the fiercest fighting and the invaders will be worn out by the time they get to the centre of the city even if they ever do". But no. The faith of Rahab conveyed itself to her family with such fervour that they put themselves in an exposed position and trusted to that scarlet cord and the honour of Israel and Israel's God.

The uncovering of Jericho in this century has thrown up some interesting discoveries. Although it is unsafe to base any belief on such an unsure foundation as modern discoveries, it appears that a part of the wall near to the town's gates did not fall down in the general collapse of the walls and it may have been here that the house of Rahab was located. How the walls of Jericho fell down we need not trouble ourselves. If they fell because of a local earthquake it is no less of a miracle that it should have happened at precisely the moment that the trumpets sounded. But Jericho fell and only Rahab and her family were saved from the otherwise total destruction.

It was into the hands of the two spies who owed their lives to Rahab that she and her family were committed. As people outside the covenant of God they were first assigned an outside place but Rahab was soon to find her place in Israel and a partaker of the divine covenant. Despite the protestations of modern rabbinical scholars who dislike the idea of a harlot being in their royal line, she became the wife of Salmon (was he one of the spies who owed his life to her?) and thus was one of the channels through whom came David, the great king of Israel (Ruth 4:21).

But much more, she was one of the channels through whom the Christ, the Son of God was to come. She is one of the five women who are named or referred to in the first chapter of Matthew which gives the "legal" descent of the Lord Jesus, showing Him to be of the line of David and Prince of the tribe of Judah. It is not without significance that each of the women in that chronology might be accused (in two cases quite unjustly) of loose living. The earthly line was a human one with all human faults and frailties, but the One who was to come at the end of that line was One who was "in all points tempted like as we are yet without sin". Rahab joins the list of women at whom the accusing finger has been pointed but to whom the words could be applied, "Neither do I condemn you ... go now and leave your life of sin" (Jn.8:11).

Because of her faith, Rahab finds herself as one of the only two women whose names are recorded in that gallery of worthies, Hebrews 11. The other is Sarah, the wife of Abraham the father of the faithful. How many other women of faith could we not have found in the Old Testament? But of them all, God has chosen Rahab the harlot to be set alongside the motherly Sarah, the only woman whose age at death is recorded and whose son mourned her passing for over two years. Because of her faith, Rahab is named by James as one who showed by her works that her faith was not a dead one (Jas.2:25). In no way does the doctrine of justification by faith conflict with James' doctrine of works. As one has said, "We are saved by faith alone but not by a faith which is alone". Faith and works are two sides of the same coin. Faith towards God and works towards men.

How much can we not learn from the life and faith of Rahab? Don't too readily point the finger at her. Remember that all the other fingers are pointing at you.

# CHAPTER SEVEN: FAITH THAT SAVES (FRED MCCORMICK)

"WE ARE NOT OF THEM that shrink back unto perdition; but of them that have faith unto the saving of the soul" (Hebrews 10.39). In the Epistle to the Hebrews there are two main lines of teaching that we will explore:

(1) The imperative necessity of those who have found a place among God's pilgrim people to go forward by faith, and hold fast that which they have in patient endurance in view of the recompense of reward.

(2) The full provision made by God for the sustenance and encouragement of the true Hebrews, or passers over, throughout the wilderness journey, through the gracious and beneficent ministry of the Great High Priest in heaven on their behalf, and also in acting as a Public Minister of the sanctuary in the presentation of their offerings as a worshipping people.

The teaching of the Epistle to the Hebrews is in striking contrast to that of the opening chapters of Ephesians. There we are seen unconditionally blessed with every spiritual blessing in Christ, quickened, raised, and seated with Him in the heavenlies. In Hebrews we see a people in the wilderness travelling onward to a better country, and on a journey, engaged in the services of God's house. In Hebrews it is not so much what we are in Him, but what we are in ourselves with our inherent weaknesses, and beset with perils, pitfalls, and snares in our pilgrim pathway, yet with God as our all-sufficient Resource.

The warnings and danger signals in the Hebrew epistle are solemn and real, and are worthy of our close attention, for every pilgrim has a life to be saved or lost. Let us mention but a few. There is e danger of drifting away from "the things that were heard and neglecting "so great salvation" (2:1-3); of becoming hardened by the deceitfulness of sin (3:13); of developing an evil heart of unbelief (3:12); of coming short of entering into God's rest (4:1); of remaining babes, and failing to press on to full growth (5:12,13); of falling away, and becoming unfruitful (6:6-8); of becoming sluggish or slothful (6:12); of forsaking the assembling of themselves together (10:25); and of being carried away by divers and strange teachings (13:9). These are a few of the many dangers mentioned as besetting God's people in this world.

These people are passing through hostile territory to their heavenly country. All their resources and strength are in heaven, their glorious Captain is there He is their "gone in" and "coming out" Hope. This world is to them as it was to David, "a dry and weary land where no water is.' They are just as dependent upon God to supply their spiritual needs as Israel were for the supply of their physical needs. Unlike Israel these people have no visible manifestations such as the pillar of fire, and of cloud, which abode upon Jehovah's dwelling place in the past, no visible priest. These people are to walk by faith, and by faith they are to overcome.

They are to give the more earnest heed to the things that were spoken by Him who is far better than angels, better than Aaron, and better than Moses. These things concerned our great salvation, which not only embraces our eternal deliverance from the consequences of sin, but also the present salvation of the soul or life, and the future salvation from sin's presence. Much of Hebrews is taken up with the salvation of the soul or life, hence the word "How shall we escape, if we neglect so great salvation?" (Hebrew's 2.2,3), and this, in the light of Hebrews

10.30,31, makes this matter one of great solemnity, for "The Lord shall judge His people. It is a fearful thing to fall into the hand of the living God.

There is, then, a life which may be saved or lost, a life made up of day-by-day experiences as the believer journeys homeward. To save it, we must walk by faith and not by sight. The Hebrews had begun well, and are exhorted to remember the former days in which, after they were enlightened, they endured a great conflict of sufferings, bearing reproaches and afflictions, and took joyfully the spoiling of their possessions, knowing that they had a better possession, and an abiding one (Heb.10:32-34).

In their joyous suffering for Christ's sake, they were also laying up treasure in heaven. It was put to their credit in the accounts of heaven, and they would find it in a coming day. Their boldness was a precious thing which had great recompense of reward, but they were now in danger of losing it by neglect. The exhortations in Hebrews encourage us to go on to the end in faith. This is essential if we are to maintain fellowship with God and our house of God position, and ultimately arrive at the end of the journey with a saved life. Note the words:

"Whose house are we, if we hold fast ... firm unto the end" (Heb.3:6).

"We are become partakers (or partners) of Christ, if we hold fast ... firm unto the end" (Heb.3.14).

"Shew the same diligence unto the fulness of hope even to the end" (Heb.6:11).

"Let us hold fast the confession of our hope that it waver not" (Heb.10:28).

In chapter 11, we have a great cloud of witnesses who "died in faith." They continued to the end, and died in expectancy. They will not be disappointed, for "God is faithful." In chapter 12 we are told to "run with patience the race set before us, looking unto Jesus, the Author and Perfecter of faith." Of Him prophetically it is written, "I have set the LORD always before me" (Ps.6:8) and "The LORD GOD hath opened Mine ear, and I was not rebellious, neither turned away backward" (Is.50:5). He set His face like a flint, and went on to the end, with faith in God, and overcame (Revelation 3.21). To win the race and gain the prize we must run to the end of the course. From the foregoing it will be observed that it is possible to neglect so great salvation, also to lose our place in God's house now, and lose our souls or lives for the future.

The Hebrews, who ran so well at first, were in danger of shrinking back. The difficulties and obstacles confronting them may have seemed well-nigh insurmountable, and almost beyond human endurance, hope was becoming dim, and the temptation to give up was ever present. This, too, has been the position of many other pilgrims since that day. What is the antidote for this condition of things? It is a sad spectacle to see all lost within sight of the goal.

"Ye hone need of patience, that, hasing done the will of God, ye may receive the promise." This life is not only an obstacle race, but is also an endurance test. "Cast not away, therefore, your boldness, which hath great recompense of reward." Abraham, having patiently endured, obtained the promise. He never gave up, he clung tenaciously to the word of God in spite of the seeming impossibility of fulfilment from the human standpoint.

"Where reason fails with all her powers, There faith prevails and love adores." Let us press on, "For yet a very little while, He that cometh shall come, and shall not tarry." "Behold I come quickly; and My reward is with Me." Meanwhile "My righteous one shall live by faith: and if he shrink back My soul hath no pleasure in him." "Now faith is the assurance of things hoped for, the proving of things not seen." The unseen eternal things are more real to faith than those visible to mortal eyes. They are the abiding realities of our heavenly inheritance and country to which we are hastening.

The Lord's pleasure is in His willing and obedient people (see Song of Songs 6:12, RV margin). "But if he shrink back My soul hath no pleasure in him." Alas, there is the sad possibility of disciples "looking back, shrinking back and going back (see Lk.9:62, Jn.8:66). "But we are not of them that shrink back unto perdition (to a wasted or lost life), but of them that have faith unto the saving of the soul" (Heb.10:39) The saving of the soul or life of a believer is something left entirely to his choice. The life cannot be saved apart from continued steadfastness in faith and obedience, and apart from this the believer will not escape the consequences of his neglect, and will therefore suffer loss of reward in relation to his works in a day to come. This is intensely solemn for us all.

The infinite sacrifice of Calvary reveals the mighty cost of our redemption, and this involves the recipients of such love in an indebtedness which is beyond our highest powers to repay. "Love that transcends our highest powers, Demands our heart, our life, our all." Far from giving to the utmost limits of our capabilities, it is often true that those things which are demanded of us are often spent in the gratification of the self-life. Time, talents, money, may be expended in worldly pleasure, while the Lord's service is neglected because of lack of these very things.

The Lord's own words are definite in demanding unreserved discipleship. In Matthew 10:38,39, He speaks of the obligations of discipleship relative to earthly relationships. The words are searching.

Discipleship demands loyalty to the Lord above all family claims, and this involves the disciple in taking up his cross to follow his Lord. Again in Mark 8.31 He began to teach them that "the Son of man must suffer ... be rejected ... and be killed." Then he says, "If any man would come after Me, let him deny himself, and take up his cross, and follow Me. For whosoever would save his life (soul, RV margin) shall lose it; and whosoever shall lose his life for My sake and the gospel's shall save it. For what doth it profit a man, to gain the whole world, and forfeit his life (or soul)?" (verses 34-40).

From this passage it is clear that to be possessed of the whole world, and yet lose or forfeit one's life, is to incur a grievous loss. Believers may here get a right sense of values. To grasp the present, or save your life now, in the sense of using this world to the full, getting out of it all you can, and putting into it all you can, means that you forfeit your life, in God's reckoning, with nothing to your account at the judgement seat of Christ, which means eternal loss.

On the contrary, those who are prepared to sacrifice the present for the future, who confess that "we have not here an abiding city," who "go forth unto Him without the camp," and are prepared to take up their cross daily, and die daily to self and earthly things, for His sake and the gospel's, these, who lose their lives here, will find them in that day (see Heb.10.34). The disciple's cross is not imposed upon him. It is not the weight of trouble and sorrow he may meet in life in common with all men. It is something he must take up of his own voluntary choice, the instrument by which he is put to death to everything contrary to his Master's will.

This requires the exercise of faith, for this course is altogether contrary to the inclinations of human nature. It requires the disciple to count "the things that are not, as though they were." By faith giving substance to the things hoped for; counting Him faithful who has promised, the disciple has to go forward to things not seen as yet, with nothing more than God's word of promise. "Abraham, when he was called, obeyed ... he went out not knowing whither he went"; it was sufficient that God had spoken.

The measure in which we are prepared to take up our cross, and lose our lives, is the measure in which we truly gain our lives for God. We need to remind ourselves that what we weave in time we wear in eternity. The saving of the soul is a matter of great importance to the believer, and in order to do this believers are exhorted to receive with meekness the implanted word which is able to save your souls" (Jas.1:18-22). By so doing, it is possible to "work out your own salvation with fear and trembling" (Phil.2:12).

Again, "as sojourners and pilgrims," we are to "abstain from fleshly lusts, which war against the soul" (1 Pet.2:11). The inworking of the flesh in the believer, exciting and prompting to fleshly lusts, will, if allowed, destroy the believer's life. "But if by the Spirit ye mortify the deeds of the body, ye shall live" (Rom.8:18). Another danger to the heavenly pilgrims is to become discouraged and weary because of the way, and hence the exhortation, "Consider Him ... that ye was not weary, fainting in your souls" (Heb.12:8).

He endured, despising shame, and has entered into glory. Our Captain, perfected through sufferings, has left us an example of patient endurance. True, the disciple pathway may be as the poet has said: "Gain'st storm, and wind, and tide." In this world there is neither sustenance, nor abiding place for true pilgrims. "Marvel not, brethren, if the world hateth you" (1 Jn.3:18). A servant is not above his Master. If we pursue the path of faith in separation to God, the world will give us the outside place as it gave to Him. Yea, and all that would live godly in Christ Jesus shalt suffer persecution" (2 Tim.3:12).

If such be the position, what then are our resources? We who are "heirs of the promise," who "shall inherit salvation," have all our resources in Him who has gone into God's presence for us as the Forerunner, within the veil. He is our "gone in" Hope. Abraham received God's promise which was confirmed by an oath; that is, he received the seed, Isaac, in whom all the promises of God were bound up, and upon his obedience of faith also received him back in a parable from the dead. And God hath sworn, "In blessing I will bless thee ... I will multiply thy seed, thy seed shall possess the gates of his enemies ... in thy seed shall all the nations of the earth be blessed; because thou hast obeyed My voice" (Gen.22.16-18; Heb.8:18-16).

The promise is confirmed by oath and is final; all the promises concerning the future were in connection with the promised seed. Likewise, God has been minded to show unto us the immutability of His counsel in regard to His promises which are bound up in the Person of the Lord Jesus Christ. He has interposed with an oath, for He has not only "witnessed of Him," but has also sworn concerning Him "The Lord sware and will not repent Himself, Thou art a Priest for ever" (Heb.7:21).

He lives in the power of an endless life, beyond the reach of any power to annul a single promise made in Him. He has entered into that which is within the veil. In Him we have the certainty and pledge of the fulfilment of every promise. To faith, this fact is as an anchor of the soul, a hope both sure and stedfast; here the believer can find all his resources as he patiently pursues the path of obedience here below. In view of those two immutable things in which it is impossible for God to lie, His promise and oath, we have a strong encouragement to lay hold of this hope.

The eternal, unseen things become positive realities to faith, and the succour, help, strength and grace for every need are supplied from this unseen source of the believer's light and life. The dangers of the pilgrim path may be great, the storms may blow upon our frail barques as we cross the sea of time, but so long as our faith, which is like the line or chain attached to the anchor within the veil, holds, we shall not drift, or make shipwreck.

It is clear then, that while our eternal security rests entirely upon the finished work of Christ, being justified by faith, saved by grace through faith, our day-by-day lives can only be saved for God if we continue to exercise faith and obedience unto the end. On God's part, every provision has been made for the journey, a throne of grace, and a Great High Priest to minister to all our necessities, yet, all these gracious provisions will not avail, unless, on our part, those "things that were heard" are mixed with faith, and we avail ourselves of those resources which will enable us to continue unto the end in the fulfilment of true discipleship.

It is ours patiently to endure throughout this little while "as seeing Him who is invisible," content to take our place with Him "outside the camp, bearing His reproach." Thus, and only thus, can we save our lives, and be numbered with the overcomers (Rev.3:21). "Wherefore let them also that suffer according to the will of God commit their souls in well-doing unto a faithful Creator" (1 Pet.4:19). Then the words will be true of us, "We are not of them that shrink back unto perdition; (or utter loss, or waste of life); but of them that have faith unto the saving of the soul."

# CHAPTER EIGHT: PERSONAL FAITH (JOHN MILLER)

---

AS TO WHETHER THE LAME man at the door of the temple called Beautiful, had faith in the Lord or not, the words of Peter in Acts 3:16 are quite clear. When Peter said, "What I have, that give I thee. In the name of Jesus Christ of Nazareth, walk" (verse 6), it is evident that the lame man received by faith and acted upon the command of Peter given in the name of Jesus Christ. Peter's words show from where the power of healing came.

"By (Greek: 'Epi', upon, 'on the ground of,' RV margin) faith in His name hath His name made this man strong, whom ye behold and know: yea, the faith which is through Him hath given him this perfect soundness in the presence of you all" (verse 16). Quite evidently the man was not only healed in body, he was also healed in soul as well, for it is said of him, that "he entered with them into the temple, walking, and leaping, and praising God. And all the people saw him walking and praising God" (verses 8, 9).

The experience of the man who lay by the pool of Bethesda (John 5) seems different from this. In his case he believed in the Lord's word though he did not know who the Speaker was. He explained the hopelessness of his state in that he had no one to help him and he had always been frustrated by another stepping down into the pool before him. Upon this the Lord said to him, "Arise, take up thy bed, and walk. And straightway the man was made whole, and took up his bed and walked" (verse 8). The man took the Lord's word as the means of healing and not the pool. For long he had looked to the story about the curative properties of the water at certain seasons, but now he looked to another source of healing and was healed immediately. But it is clear that he did not know who spoke to him. Later the Lord found him in the temple and said to him, "Behold, thou art made whole: sin no more, lest a worse thing befall thee. The man went away, and told the Jews that it was Jesus which had made him whole" (verses 14,15). Consequent upon this the Jews persecuted the Lord. Though the man believed the Lord's word there seems to be no evidence that he believed in the Lord Himself. We conclude that he knew healing of the body, but not of the soul. This seems to emerge in the meaning of this sign.

In the case of the blind man in John 9, we have another kind of experience. Here was a blind man who was told by the Lord, after He had made clay with spittle and anointed his blind eyes, to go to the Pool of Siloam and wash. He also did not know who the Lord was, but he received by faith the Lord's word and acted upon it. His simple, straightforward account of his experience was, "He put clay upon mine eyes, and I washed; and do see" (verse 15). Though the receiving of sight by the blind man was instantaneous, his knowledge of who was the Lord was gradual. To the question of the Pharisees, "What sayest thou of Him, in that He opened thine eyes? And he said, He is a prophet" (verse 17).

He had made a true assessment of the Lord from one point of view, for a prophet was a man who spoke God's message, whether to a man, as in the case of Naaman the Syrian by Elisha, or to Israel by Elijah, and on many other occasions. The Lord had a message for the blind man, but He was much more than a prophet. The blind man accepted the Lord's word as a message to him from God. Later the accusation of the Pharisees that the Lord was a sinner was repelled by the blind man. He propounded a truth of both Old and New Testaments when he said, "We know that God heareth not sinners: but if any man be a worshipper of God, and do His will, him He heareth. Since the world began it was never heard that any one opened the eyes of a man born blind. If this Man were not from God, He could do nothing" (verses 31-33).

When the Pharisees had cast the once blind man out of the synagogue and the Lord had found him, the Lord asked him, "Dost thou believe on the Son of God?" He did not know who He was, so he said, 'Who is He, Lord, that I may believe on Him?" Upon this the Lord said, "Thou hast both seen Him, and He it is that speaketh with thee. And he said, Lord, I believe. And he worshipped Him." Appreciation of who was the Lord, was gradual, though the revelation of His divine Sonship was at once.

That some were healed bodily through the faith of others, is beyond question, as seen in the case of the nobleman's son (Jn.4:46-54), the centurion's servant (Lk.7:2-10), and the Canaanite woman's daughter who was demon-possessed (Matt.15:21-28). But where the question of the forgiveness of sins and eternal salvation is involved, in conjunction with the healing of the body, personal faith in Christ is in evidence, as in the case of the palsied man, in Luke 5:17-26, for "seeing their faith, He said, Man, thy sins are forgiven thee," that is, the faith of the man and his four friends. The Lord forgiving sins is only mentioned once again in the Gospels, when He forgave the woman, a sinner in the city, in Simon the Pharisee's house. He said, "Thy sins are forgiven," and again Thy faith hath saved thee; go in peace" (Lk.7:36-50). No one is eternally saved by proxy or because of another's faith, but believing prayer by believers on behalf of others is undoubtedly heard by God, but those, however much they may be prayed for, must exercise personal faith in the Lord in order to be saved.

# CHAPTER NINE: FAITH IN ACTION – CALEB (ALAN TOMS)

**FAITH TO CONQUER**

The first time we read of Caleb is in Numbers 13 when he was chosen as one of the princes to spy out the land. He represented his tribe, Judah. He was a prince by nature as well as by rank; a princely man of faith. Like his ten brethren, he also saw the great stature of the people of the land and their fenced cities. He saw the giants too. But he saw beyond, for faith always takes a long-distance view. He saw the Lord who had promised to give them the land and was waiting to fulfil His promise.

"If the LORD delight in us, then He will bring us into this land, and give it unto us" (Num.14:8). That was the 'if' of argument, not of doubt. There was no question that the Lord delighted in them. Had He not delivered them from the tyranny of Egypt, divided the Red Sea, fed them with daily manna and provided a pillar of fire and cloud to guide them by night and day? The whole matter was as clear as daylight to Caleb's faith and he stood courageously by his convictions, even at the risk of being stoned. "Trust ye in the LORD for ever: for in the LORD JEHOVAH is an everlasting rock" (Is.26:4). This man of faith stood firm as a rock!

**Faith to Endure**

We do not read of him again until they came into the land and once more he was chosen as one of the princes to assist in dividing it up. Joshua his companion now occupied a more eminent role, as the new leader of God's people, but there was no jealousy on Caleb's part. How do we know? Because he wholly followed the Lord. Moses had said so, but better than that, God said so, and more than once. And God knew his heart. He wholly followed. The word is an interesting one. It carries the thought of being full. His life was literally filled with following the Lord. Had he given place in his heart to any jealousy he would have forfeited that high commendation of the Lord.

**Faith to Possess**

On his eighty-fifth birthday he presented himself to Joshua with the request that he be allocated mount Hebron as his possession. He had set his heart on it forty-five years before when he spied out the land. "Give me this mountain", he said in a soul stirring burst of conquering faith (Josh.14:12). The Anakim were there, the greatest among the giants. But those giants who filled the hearts of his brethren with terror, served only as a challenge to this man's faith. His heart rested on a word from God. "I shall drive them out, as the LORD spake" he said. For forty-five years he had cherished that word. His faith had relied on it. And he did drive them out. The next chapter records the conquest and Caleb spent the closing years of his life in Hebron fellowship with God.

That had been the order of his life, of course. He wholly followed the Lord. Day by day he walked with Him through all those years in the desert. He quietly walked with God. Lesser men might have held a bitterness in their hearts, but not Caleb. Had it not been for his brethren's unbelief he might have enjoyed the blessings of the land all those years. But it would seem that he did not allow such thoughts to distress him unduly. For he said he was as strong at eighty-five years of age as he was at forty, and did not express any bitterness about the long years in the wilderness. Bitterness in the heart, or a grudge, damage the person who holds it far more than the one against whom it is directed. Therefore "let all bitterness, and wrath, and anger, and clamour, and railing, be put away from you, with all malice: and be ye kind one to another, tenderhearted, forgiving each other, even as God also in Christ forgave you" (Eph.4:31,32). Caleb seemed to live by that rule.

"They that wait upon the LORD shall renew their strength." That was the secret of Caleb's strength. "They shall mount up with wings as eagles" and so he did, at Kadesh-barnea and again at Hebron. Faith soared high on those occasions. But what of those thirty-eight long years in the waste and howling wilderness? Surely those years were an even greater test of his faith. They were. But "they that wait upon the LORD ... shall run, and not be weary; they shall walk and not faint." Caleb proved the truth of that word. Shall we not be encouraged by his faith and ask the Lord's help to do the same?

# CHAPTER TEN: JUSTIFICATION BY FAITH AND BY WORKS (JACK FERGUSON)

THESE ARE TWO WEIGHTY matters. Briefly, justification by faith has to do with the salvation of the sinner. Justification by works has to do with the believer subsequently doing what is right in his life day by day in the service of the Lord.

A sinner is initially justified by the hearing of faith, not by the works of the law, whether it be the law of God or that of any other code of conduct. Romans 4 and Galatians 3 explain this fully. Yet on this subject there is much confusion of thought. The guidance from God is clear. One particularly helpful verse is Ephesians 2:8, "For by grace have ye been saved through faith; and that not of yourselves: it is the gift of God: not of works, that no man should glory". What could be clearer?

But the plain sense of these words has been distorted and indeed negatived by the systematic teaching of great ecclesiastical movements. A former Primus of the Scottish Church, a man of deep personal piety, wrote, "We go into the Church, we are brought into the Church - when at the font baptized, and made members of Christ, children of God, and heirs of the Kingdom of Heaven". Whereas the real truth is simply put by John the apostle, writing of the days of the Lord's coming into the world, "He came unto His own, and they that were His own received Him not. But as many as received Him, to them gave He the right to become children of God, even to them that believe on His name" (Jn.1:11,12).

Further, it is evident today that vast numbers of our relatives, neighbours and business associates consider that deeds of merit, of whatever kind, will ensure for them a place in the saints' everlasting rest. The deeds themselves are not to be despised. But the fearful consequences of the false hopes they engender call for incessant exposure. The so-called Christian nations need again the clarion call of the 16th century Reformers, back again to the scriptural requirement of justification by grace and faith in Christ alone.

Some of the historians of the early Christian era have noted that in those primal years there was a growing disinclination on the part of the converts to give themselves to a life of good works after conversion. Increasing stress was therefore laid by their teachers on the need for good works. Gradually, however, grace and goods works began to share in emphasis and finally personal merit displaced grace altogether. Hence, in due course, the Reformation took shape.

You may remember the account of how Luther, shortly after entering the monastery at Erfurth, fell seriously ill, and an aged brother-monk came to his bedside and began to repeat, with much simplicity and earnestness, the Apostles' Creed, "I believe in the forgiveness of sins". As Luther in feeble accents repeated the words after him, a ray of light entered his darkened mind. "He saw it all; the whole gospel in a single phrase, the forgiveness of sins not the payment but the forgiveness". Yes, "The just shall live by faith".

A large number of people have a totally unscriptural perspective in spiritual matters. They regard good works as leading into salvation, whereas God describes the good works of a person before conversion as "dead works" (see Heb.6:1, 9:14). Yet many of us who are enjoying the assurance of justification by faith alone may well be seriously at fault in another way. We may be forgetting that good works should follow salvation. They are integral to the divine plan of human redemption.

The Scriptures evidencing this are too many to set out here. Notable among them is Ephesians 2:10. It describes those who have been justified by faith apart from works. "For we are His workmanship, created in Christ Jesus for good works, which God afore prepared that we should walk in them". So that not only did He plan our salvation before times eternal, but in the plan He provided for the new life to make itself manifest in good works.

This essential aspect of the Christian life is expanded by James in chapter 2 of his epistle. He terms it justification by works, describes it in operation in the lives of such different characters as Abraham and Rahab, and views it as the outworking of a saving faith, without which practical expression faith would be dead, inoperative, unfruitful. The new life in the believer should be evidenced in good works. God expects them, the Lord Jesus practised them, the people of God are to be zealous in them, Dorcas was full of them, the wealthy are to be rich in them, the widows in Paul's day were diligently to follow them, the man of God is to be furnished completely in them, and in the day of visitation those around us are to be able to glorify God by reason of them.

The Thessalonian church was commended for its "work of faith". A life of good works proceeds from the vision of faith whereby the disciple endeavours to see surrounding need as the Lord sees it, who makes His sun to rise on the evil and the good. The channels are manifold. There is the call to steadfast continuance in the services of the assembly. There are home responsibilities to be pursued with diligence. There are the spiritual needs of the perishing with whom we come in contact, young and old. There are the lonely to be visited, prayed with, read to; the sorrowing to be comforted; the sick to be tended; the poor it may be to be fed. There are letters of sympathy or of encouragement to be sent.

And what of opportunities for entertaining (it may even be of angels unawares). Little things as some might view them, but great to Him and to the beneficiary.

We live in an atmosphere today which is charged with self-interest, time-absorbing employment, pressures of all sorts which would edge out of our lives, out of our high calling, out of so great salvation, the good works which God afore prepared that we should walk in them. Many are alerted to this and we write for their encouragement in an unappreciative day. Others may not be so and we write for their stimulus. How did our fathers manage it? Some of us look back on the elders of our earlier years. The men had long hours at work and the women, too, in their non-labour-saving homes; they walked or used public transport. Yet they left behind them an impression of care for others amid it all. Well did the Holy Spirit say, "and considering the issue of their life, imitate their faith" (Heb.13:7). "And God is able to make all grace abound unto you; that ye, having always all sufficiency in everything, may abound unto every good work" (2 Cor. 9:8). And the poet has written:

How far in service must I go,

What sacrifices bring

To God, whose loving hands bestow

Each good and perfect thing?

How much of time and thought should I

Devote to Him who died?

What is my debt to Him and why,

And how, may I decide?

A measured service bound would be

A service mean and small.

He did not ask "how much?" from me,

He gave Himself, His all.

He did not ask how far to go;

How far was not to say

What bound? How far? I only know

That He went all the way.

# CHAPTER ELEVEN: THE SACRIFICE AND SERVICE OF FAITH (GUY JARVIE)

"IF I AM OFFERED UPON the sacrifice and service of your faith, I joy, and rejoice with you all" (Phil.2:17). Paul is here referring to the drink offering which was offered with other offerings (the burnt offering and the peace offering) (see Num.15.1-11). He likens the losing of his life to the drink offering. A life that is not sacrificed for Christ is a lost life, and a life that is not spent in acceptable service to God is also a futile and wasted life. But only faith will enable us to lose our lives for Christ's sake and the gospel's sake.

Everywhere around us our fellow men are living for themselves and for worldly pleasure and advancement. They are tersely described in the Scriptures as "lovers of self, lovers of money" (2 Tim.3:2). This attitude of mind is so universal, that the disciple is an odd man in the world. Because of this world-feeling of selfishness, the young disciple often has a struggle to gain his feet in the life of faith. He sees so many who are living for themselves, that he finds it difficult to yield his own life unreservedly to the Lord, to walk by faith.

However, a little logical thinking will balance the mind of the disciple. Compared with eternity, this life is very short indeed, and whatever a man may get for himself during this life, he can take nothing with him. In the concise reasoning of Paul, "We brought nothing into the world, for neither can we carry anything out" (1 Tim.6:7). That is sound logic! Then also the pleasures of this life are often marred by sickness and disappointment. Those who set out to please themselves are often the most frustrated people. Even those who do social or humanitarian work for others, have more joy and satisfaction in life than the lovers of self and lovers of money.

But the disciple of the Lord Jesus is not merely a humanitarian worker, although he should be zealous in good works. The first claim upon his life is not of humanity. It is the claim of Christ, the claim of the nail-pierced Hands. We may live unto ourselves, or we may live unto Christ. That is the choice before us. Sacrifice comes before service, or, rather, true service is sacrifice. It is the yielded life, the life of faith. Service which is not sacrificial is without value, and sacrifice which is not the result of faith and love is equally valueless.

Young disciple, the Lord Jesus claims your life to use it as He will. Are you willing to give it to Him? Are you willing to lose it in the sacrifice and service of faith? You may have certain ambitions in your life. Are you willing to surrender all your ambitions for a greater ambition, the ambition to be well-pleasing to Christ? (2 Cor.5.9). Your earthly ambitions may be perfectly right, but being earthly, they can only last for the short period of the present life.

So there lies before you a sacrifice and service which can only be seen by faith. No one can tell you what this sacrifice and service will mean for you, but you can certainly trust the Lord to use your life in the best way, whether it be at home or abroad. You will find as you step out in the sacrifice and service of faith, that the way will open before you, for the work that the Lord has for you. He knows what you can do, better than you do yourself. You will see His leading, both by the urge upon your own spirit, and by the circumstances of life.

Do not be deceived by the empty futile lives of those who live for themselves. The joy they have in their way of life is short-lived, for God has decreed that vanity will follow their steps (Eccl.11:9,10; Rom.8:20). Step out by faith, and the worth-while life, the life indeed, will be your portion, now and for eternity.

# CHAPTER TWELVE: FAITH IN ACTION – TWO GENTILES (JOHN MILLER)

IT IS A REMARKABLE thing that the two people whose faith the Lord described as great were both Gentiles, strangers to the covenants of the promise. In both cases their great faith in the Lord was exercised on the behalf of others, persons that were very dear to them; in the case of the Centurion, in Matthew 8:5-8, it was on behalf of his servant, and in that of the Canaanite woman it was for her daughter (Matthew 15:21-28). One can almost think that the Lord is finding relief for His spirit in these incidents in an otherwise dry and barren soil in Israel, largely destitute of faith, and is beginning to move toward the realization of the eternal purpose of His heart to bring in the Gentiles into blessing from which they had been so long alienated.

The same thought emerges in the book of Malachi. The remnant that had returned from Babylon and had rebuilt God's house, and had raised the wall of Jerusalem and set up the gates thereof, did not long evince the enthusiasm of the early days of this divine movement. The sons of the men who had left Babylon, and trudged the long weary miles over the desert to reach the land of promise, were, alas, not of the spiritual qualities of their fathers. Theirs was an easier life and a more sinful one, and they had descended to that low level, that anything would do for God. Cattle which their governor would not eat were good enough to be burnt on the altar of God. But God reminded the unworthy priests that there were others beyond the land of Israel who thought more worthily of Him. He says, "From the rising of the sun even unto the going down of the same My name is great among the Gentiles; and in every place incense is offered unto My name, and a pure offering: for My name is great among the Gentiles, saith the LORD of Hosts" (Mal.1:11).

This statement by the LORD did not mean that He was at that time breaking His covenant with His people, the remnant which were in the place of the name in Jerusalem, and that He was moving out to the Gentile nations. It is the responsibility of all men to bow and adore their Divine Creator. The terms of the everlasting gospel call for this: "Fear God, and give Him glory; and worship Him that made the heaven and the earth and sea and fountains of waters" (Rev.14:7). And Peter said in the house of Cornelius, "a truth I perceive that God is no respecter of persons: But in every nation he that feareth Him and worketh righteousness is acceptable to Him" (Acts 10:34,35). The outworking of this statement of divine truth was seen in the actions of Cornelius, whose prayers and almsgiving had ascended for a memorial before God.

We do not know how many there may be in whom God finds pleasure, and it ill becomes the remnant of His people to-day to drift into a proud and careless condition, as the remnant were in Malachi's day or their descendants four hundred years afterwards in the Lord's time when religions hypocrisy wrought like a plague amongst the Israel people. God has no place for religious humbug, and in the Lord's time the movement was under way of reaching out to that world which God loved with so great love that He gave His only begotten Son.

In that chapter (Hebrews 11) in which Paul recounts the triumphs of faith, he speaks of Enoch's life of faith as being well-pleasing to God, and says that "without faith it is impossible to be well-pleasing unto Him." The great faith of the Centurion in Matthew 8, and of the Canaanite woman in Matthew 15, must have been a joy to the Lord. Pride and faith are antagonistic to each other and they cannot lodge in peace in the same heart. Faith is trustful and dependent, pride is self-reliant and independent. Think of what the Centurion said: "Lord, I am not worthy that Thou shouldest come under my roof: but only say the word, and my servant shall be healed" (Matt.8:8).

To whom was he speaking? To One who said that the foxes had holes and the birds of the air their nests, but He had nowhere to lay His head. The Centurion is not viewing the Lord's greatness by a comparison of homes or of what they each possessed. He looked far beyond the confines of material wealth and worldly circumstance. He saw in the Man of Galilee One of infinite power, whose worth demanded for Him the rainbow-circled throne of heaven, though He but yesterday had left the toil of the carpenter's bench and the lowly home in Nazareth.

True greatness is not in what one has but in what one is. What you have is moveable, but what you are is permanent. Whom did the Centurion address? It was the Lord and that was enough. If He was the Lord then authority of an infinite kind was His. "Only say the word," said he, "and my servant shall be healed." "The word" is vital to faith. Faith cometh by hearing, and hearing by the word of God, we are told.

"Abba, Father, all things are possible unto Thee" (Mk.14:36) finds a counterpart in "All things are possible to Him that believeth" (Mk.9:28). Almighty power and depending faith make possible the impossible. And so it was in the Centurion's case, for the Lord said, "Go thy way; as thou hast believed, so be it done unto thee. And the servant was healed in that hour." Oh, to have greater reliance on the Lord's spoken word!

Also in the case of the Canaanite woman we see clearly that pride and great faith cannot lodge together. "She came and worshipped Him, saying, Lord help me" (Matt.15:26). He spoke to her as she lay at His feet that it was not right to take the children's bread and cast it to the dogs. The "Son of David," as she addressed Him, had come to find and tend the flock that David had cared for. She was an outsider. But she would take the place of the little dogs, if perchance she might receive a crumb of mercy from the table of Israel that the Lord had so lavishly furnished in His mercy, and which by the most part was despised. Her humility was great, but not too great. Great humility and great faith reposed within her. The Lord said to her, "O woman, great is thy faith!" The mercy she sought was hers, for her daughter was healed that hour.

Pride and self-trust are seen in the Pharisee of Luke 18, but humility and faith in the publican, and the Lord's words about these two and others remain true about all who are like them: "I say unto you, This man (the publican) went down to his house justified rather than the other: for every one that exalteth himself shall be humbled; but he that humbleth himself shall be exalted" (Lk.18:14).

A proud sinner cannot be saved, and faith cannot grow in the hearts of proud saints. But "why should the spirit of mortals be proud?"

# CHAPTER THIRTEEN: FAITH AND DOUBT (JACK GAULT)

I HAVE OFTEN WONDERED why it should be that Christians pass through times of doubt. I submit that there may be several reasons for this. Our faith is centred upon our Lord Jesus Christ, and, although we believe on Him, we have never seen Him. His life and death, burial and resurrection are all important to our faith as being those things which declare Him to be the Son of God and the Saviour of the world, yet the majority refuse to accept that these events ever took place. The world in which we live is in the main hostile to our faith and our beliefs. The fundamentals of the Faith are disputed, disbelieved and denied. The mass media are in the main aligned to anti-Christian thinking so that our faith is under constant bombardment from the things we see and hear.

Furthermore, the Bible, the main channel of revelation and the source of great comfort to all believers day by day, is not generally regarded as the inspired Word of God. It is considered by many not to have the authority which Christians ascribe to it. In our own personal lives too, sickness, hardship, bereavement and other unpleasant experiences, although the common lot of all mankind, can cause Christians to doubt the things they hold most dear. To have times of doubt therefore seems inevitable, and one might consider whether it is not, in the will of God, meant to be a necessary discipline for us: part of the process of growing "in the grace and knowledge of our Lord and Saviour Jesus Christ".

When considering the subject of doubt one inevitably thinks of Thomas the apostle on that occasion when the Lord first appeared to His disciples after His resurrection. For some reason not explained to us Thomas was not present. Later when they told him what had happened, Thomas could not believe it. The combined testimonies of all the others failed to convince him that the Lord was indeed risen from the dead and had appeared to them. Thomas wanted to have his own personal proof and nothing else would satisfy him. This is a perfect example of doubt and disbelief. Thomas said, "Except I shall see in His hands the print of the nails, and put my finger into the print of the nails, and put my hand into His side, I will not believe" (Jn.20:25). It is reassuring, however, to notice that the Lord knew of the doubt being expressed by Thomas. A week later when He appeared a second time to the disciples, and when Thomas was present, the Lord spoke directly to him and showed to him the unmistakable evidence for which he had asked. We might ask why the Lord had kept Thomas waiting a week before clearing the doubt from his mind: a week of bewilderment and perplexity; a week of isolation in thought and experience from the other disciples before he could share in their new-found joy and confidence in the risen Lord.

Again, one thinks of Peter the apostle and of that stormy night on Lake Galilee when, as he walked on the water, he began to sink. The Lord said to him after He had stretched out His hand to save him from sinking, "O thou of little faith, wherefore didst thou doubt?" What more could Peter have asked for on that occasion? The Lord was not only present on the scene, but had also given His assent to Peter's request, "Bid me come to Thee upon the water". At the Lord's command, Peter was doing that which was humanly impossible: he was walking on the water. His faith had enabled him to begin to do so, and then he began to sink. What had gone wrong? It must have been the environment which caused Peter to lose his faith. The wind was boisterous and the sea was rough. It was dark, he was tired, and with the others he had had a fright thinking that they had seen an apparition. His faith was under attack and it was not equal to the occasion.

Perhaps in the word of the Lord to Peter, "O thou of little faith, wherefore didst thou doubt?" there is the key to the problem of doubt. It is surely the absence of faith which causes the doubt. Faith and doubt are like the opposite ends of a see-saw. When faith is riding high, doubt is low and conversely when faith is low, doubt is high. The Lord once said to His disciples, "If ye have faith and doubt not ..." (Matt.21:21) We live in an environment which is hostile to us and, like Peter, when we look at what is taking place around us we can become afraid and begin to doubt. For this reason, the fellowship of other Christians is vitally important to us and we do well not to absent ourselves from their company. Fellow Christians can help us to overcome our doubt, but there may be times when, like Thomas, we will be satisfied only with a word from the Lord.

God often does speak to us personally through His Word just as directly as the Lord spoke to Thomas. For Thomas, that wonderful moment of revelation may have produced a sense of personal shame for his lack of faith, but one thing seems certain: from that moment onwards his faith would be unshakable. Each doubt overcome and put behind us makes us stronger and more mature, yet we may never reach the end of our doubts, or our fears, until that great day when we shall, like Thomas, stand in the presence of our Lord and our God.

Perhaps, therefore, the experience of doubting is a necessary part of Christian living. We often feel that one brief outshining of the Lord's presence would be enough to banish all doubt from our minds and permit us to live the rest of our lives in unmitigated euphoria. That one brief glimpse does not come, however, and so we must wait for that glorious day of His unveiling. The Lord said to Thomas: "Because thou hast seen Me thou hast believed: blessed are they that have not seen and yet have believed" (Jn.20:29).

# CHAPTER FOURTEEN: FAITH IN ACTION – MOSES (FRED EVANS)

---

IF WE HAD NO OLD TESTAMENT it would still be possible to construct a reasonably full account of the chronological events and the important characteristics of the life of Moses from the New Testament. There are almost sixty references to him, about half in the Gospels, the rest spread through the Acts of the Apostles and the Epistles, with one in the Revelation. The ground covers the period from his birth to his death and burial, with a possible glimpse of the future. The three forty-year phases of his life are dealt with, and various outstanding incidents are referred to in some detail. Space does not permit a consideration of many references, so it becomes necessary to select a few of them. Thus we propose to confine this chapter to specific exposition of some references in the Epistle to the Hebrews.

### The Faith of his Parents

Moses, "when he was born", was cradled in the faith of his godly parents. "They saw he was a goodly (KJV 'proper') child". They apparently associated something with the child which caused them to feel that it was God's purpose to preserve and use him. It has even been suggested that they possibly had some divine revelation or word to rest on, which marked out the child as one through whom God designed to do a great work. Their resultant faith caused them to hide the child for three months. Their faith triumphed over any fear they had - "they were not afraid of the king's commandment". They endangered their own lives to preserve the life of their child (Heb.11:23).

### The Choice of Faith

This example of personal parental faith found an answering response in their son, "when he was grown up". When he was ripe for mature deliberation, he was called on to make the vital decision. On the one hand, the princely status of a son of the daughter of the royal house of Pharaoh, with the remote possibility of eventually succeeding to the throne of Egypt. A life of enjoyment of all that Egypt had to offer in the way of treasures and pleasures, with the challenge of Egypt's progressive civilization and regal opportunity. On the other hand, identification with his own people, the Hebrews, a race of slaves. A life of suffering and self-denial, sharing their hardships and reproach. But a life with and for the people of God, with a divinely ordained destiny.

Moses was called to make this choice when he was forty years old, at a time when his powers of mind and body were fully developed. He had grown ripe for enjoyment, and at an age when he was capable of relishing material luxuries and the pleasant benefits which the world had to offer. It was no hasty impulse which guided him. But for him in these circumstances the pleasures of the world and the treasures of the court were 'the pleasures of sin". He refused them. He deliberately preferred to be known publicly as one with "the people of God". He would not undervalue this true honour. These people might be a race of slaves, but to his faith they were God's chosen, "an elect race". The almighty God had His purposes for them and for him.

What strengthened Moses in making his important and far-reaching decision? His faith in the Living God. And what motivated him? "He looked unto the recompense of reward". His eyes were turned away from the short-lived comfort and luxury: they were fixed on the eternal recompense (Heb.11:24-26).

**Faith in the Invisible**

In the pathway of faith one decision often leads on to others. Moses had made his choice - to involve himself with the people of God and to suffer evil treatment. It meant leaving his mother by adoption, and setting his back on the Egyptian court. But where was he to go? He could hardly expect any of the Hebrew slaves to hide him successfully. Could he conceal himself in the tawny-yellow desert lands flanking the river Nile or in the broad delta plains? Dare he leave the country entirely, so adding insult to injury, thus incurring the king's greater antagonism? Yes, this must be his course. "By faith he forsook Egypt: not fearing the wrath of the king". Dire consequences were likely to overtake him if he should be caught after leaving Egypt in defiance of Pharaoh.

He had resolved to play his part with the oppressed Israelites, which he could not have done satisfactorily if he had decided to remain. This motive constituted his act of faith, "for he endured, as seeing Him who is invisible". His dealings were with God alone, who though invisible to his bodily eyes was ever before his "eyes of faith" (Heb.11:27).

### The Vision of Faith

The next step of faith in the life of Moses taken up by the Holy Spirit in Hebrews 11 is of rather a different nature yet a vital link in the chain. "By faith he kept (instituted) the passover, and the sprinkling of the blood, that the destroyer of the firstborn should not touch them" (v.28).

By this time Moses was quite aware of the role he was expected by God to fulfil in His purposes for His people. God had promised that the destroyer would pass over and not touch the occupiers of the blood-sprinkled houses. Moses believed God and rested on the promise. As Calvin wrote, "He acquiesced in the bare word of God where the thing itself was not apparent". His faith also helped the people to believe beforehand in the certainty of divine judgement upon the firstborn of Egypt and of divine shelter for Israel complying with the appointed provision of the sprinkled blood. But his faith went further than that.

Of the Passover, the LORD had said, "Ye shall keep it a feast to the LORD: throughout your generations ye shall keep it a feast by an ordinance for ever" (Ex.12:14). Moses again believed God and "instituted" the feast. Is it too much to suggest that faith's vision which Moses saw for his enslaved people was of a free. united and obedient people, established in a national home, regularly keeping the Passover for centuries to come? They would remember their emancipation from Egypt and their divine Emancipator in the manner of his instituting. Fifteen centuries later, the Messiah Himself was to say, "With desire I have desired to eat this passover with you before I suffer" (Lk.22:15). It was on this occasion that the Lord Jesus instituted a different memorial for His New Testament people when He said, "This do in remembrance of Me".

**Moses and Faithfulness**

The true man of faith becomes a faithful man. The two Greek words are from the same root. The person who truly believes or has a firm persuasion becomes one on whom reliance can be placed. He is worthy of trust or trustworthy and reliable. This was true of Moses - in all God's house he was faithful to God who appointed him as His servant. "My servant Moses ... is faithful in all Mine house" (Num.12:7). This was not man's testimony but that of the all-seeing and almighty God. It was and still is the witness of the only One who had complete knowledge of Moses - his character, his motives and his actions. A wonderful testimony indeed! It was spoken at the door of "the tent of meeting".

The earlier word to Moses had been emphatic and clear. "Let them make Me a sanctuary; that I may dwell among them. According to all that I show thee, the pattern of the tabernacle, and the pattern of all the furniture thereof, even so shall ye make it" (Ex.25:8,9). There was to be no introduction by Moses of any of his own ideas based on a close connection with the constructions and traditions of Egypt. Neither were there to be any modifications according to his own personal whims. The pattern had been shown him in the Mount. The actual construction of the Tabernacle and all its contents was faithfully executed under Moses' supervision according to God's pattern. Its erection and the detailed arrangements for its consecration, also administrative arrangements connected with the High Priest and the supporting priests, with their consecration - everything was done "as the LORD commanded Moses".

With this faithfulness the great Jehovah God was so satisfied that "the cloud covered the tent of meeting, and the glory of the LORD filled the tabernacle" (Ex.40:34). This was an outstanding day in the life of Moses and the people of God. The day of fulfilled desire on the part of the LORD God when He in His glory had actually come to dwell among His people. It was also a day of triumph of faith and faithfulness on the part of Moses, His meek and honoured servant.

"For Moses: he forsook the land

Where wealth and power were in his hand:

By faith the passover he kept,

Led Israel forth while Rahab wept:

We give Thee thanks."

# CHAPTER FIFTEEN: FAITH AND SPIRITUAL GROWTH (REG PARKER)

THE TONE OF THE BOOK of the Acts of the Apostles is set in the first verse. Luke's first treatise concerned all that Jesus began both to do and to teach. The next two verses imply that Luke's second treatise, the Acts of the Apostles, concerns all that Jesus continued both to do and to teach. We cannot, however, overlook the fact that the doing and teaching were no longer to be fulfilled by Jesus personally but by the apostles whom He had chosen. Delegation of this work together with the necessary authority are confirmed by Luke's record, "He was received up, after that He had given commandment through the Holy Spirit" (Acts 1:2). For this reason the title of the book is given as the Acts of the Apostles, but it is often called "The Acts of the Holy Spirit".

The Gospels therefore deal with what Jesus began both to do and to teach. The purpose of John's Gospel is clearly stated, "that ye may believe ... that believing ye may have life in His Name" (Jn.20:31). The Gospels have in view the commencement of spiritual life, whereas the Acts has greater emphasis on the continuity of spiritual life and the achievement of spiritual growth. In the Gospels and in the Acts, both spiritual life and spiritual growth rest upon a foundation of faith. They teach that spiritual life commences by faith, Spiritual life is nourished by faith, Spiritual growth is promoted by faith. Spiritual comprehension and understanding are not dependent upon education and natural birth but upon the work of the Holy Spirit, Spiritual attainment is by degrees, by steps or stages, Spiritual walk should be according to the level of attainment already achieved.

We can also show there are three fundamental principles of spiritual growth which are illustrated in the Acts as follows:

## 1. Spiritual Life Begins by Faith

There are numerous examples in the Acts where the Spirit of God worked through the apostles to give spiritual life on the basis of faith. The message of Peter on the day of Pentecost was, "it shall be, that whosoever shall call on the Name of the Lord shall be saved" (2:16,21). Paul says, "How then shall they call on Him in whom they have not believed"? (Rom.10:14). The incident of the lame man, who was daily laid at the door of the temple supports the same thought "By faith in His Name ... yea, the faith which is through Him hath given him this perfect soundness" (3:16). The rulers, elders, scribes and those of the kindred of the high priest were unable to understand this work of faith. Their perplexity is revealed by their enquiry, "By what power (Greek: 'dunamis' - ability), or in what name, have ye done this"? (4:7).

We see how spiritual life on the basis of faith was not limited to Jews, but was extended to Gentiles by the confession of the Ethiopian eunuch (8:37) and the exercise of faith by Cornelius, his kinsmen and his near friends. "Everyone that believeth on Him shall receive remission of sins" (10:43). The jailor in Philippi "believed in God" (16:34) and following Paul's visit to the Areopagus some believed (17:34). The basis of Paul's talk with King Agrippa was believing (26:27). As a result of Paul's persuasion of those who came to see him in Rome, some believed (28:23,24). Clearly the commencement of spiritual life is through faith in our Lord Jesus Christ.

## 2. Spiritual Life is Nourished by Faith

From the days of Habakkuk, living by faith (2:4) is indelibly recorded in the Scriptures, although it had been practised by all men of God before Habakkuk's day. To Paul, the Christian life was a life lived by faith as can be seen by his use of Habakkuk's statement three times. In Romans 1:17 the emphasis is on the righteous shall live by faith; when writing to the Galatians he emphasizes living by faith (3:11) and to the Hebrews (assuming that Paul wrote the epistle) he places the emphasis on faith (10:38). The spiritual life was nourished by faith resulting in those so living being numbered together as recorded by Luke, "and all that believed were together" (2:44) and again, "the multitude of them that believed were of one heart and soul" (4:32). As others who believed by faith were added to them, "they continued stedfastly in the apostles' teaching and fellowship, in the breaking of bread and the prayers" (2:41,42).

How could they be otherwise when among them we're men like Stephen, "a man full of faith" (6:5) and Barnabas who "was a good man, and full of the Holy Spirit and of faith" (11:24). Even on the verge of shipwreck Paul witnessed, "I believe God" (27:25), the very Person, "whose I am, whom also I serve" (27:23).

### 3. Spiritual Life is Promoted by Faith

We can see then, that the men and women who grew in stature for God as recorded in the Acts were those whose lives were lived by faith. Also, they did not plough lone furrows of individual experience, but there was a collective purpose in their lives. How often we hear professing Christians say there is no need to go to church; "I can worship and serve God at home". God's purpose is that lives of faith should be lived together in a collective experience seen so clearly in the Acts. There was togetherness, a oneness in witness and testimony which Luke records so faithfully. They were "together" in a sense which went far beyond merely assembling at regular intervals. They were joined together in a fellowship or partnership which accepted certain corporate obligations and responsibilities. The history of the church of God in Jerusalem reveals the unity of purpose with which those obligations and responsibilities were performed. Their present and future growth was promoted by faith.

# CHAPTER SIXTEEN: FAITH IN ACTION – JACOB (ANON)

BY FAITH JACOB, WHEN he was a dying, blessed each of the sons of Joseph; and worshipped, leaning upon the top of his staff. The writer of the epistle to the Hebrews had a profound understanding of the "things written aforetime". His knowledge of Old Testament history, and in particular of God's ways with His people Israel, shines from every page of that remarkable book. He was also deeply taught in the typology of the sacrificial system of the Old Covenant as it foreshadowed "the good things to come" of which we are now the beneficiaries.

But there was a further feature of Old Testament revelation which claimed a prominent place in his survey of the history of redemption. Interwoven in that history from its early beginnings were the exploits of men and women of faith who in their day played a vital part in its unfolding.

All who prize divine revelation as it is disclosed in the Old Testament story treasure the example of those whose names find honourable mention in Hebrews chapter 11. The list, of course, is not complete, but we can fill in the picture and gain further encouragement from the army of the unmentioned who followed "in their train". To demonstrate the faith of these worthies the writer of Hebrews focused on some outstanding incident or feat in their experiences, not that these were isolated from the general tenor of their lives, but were high peaks to which faith conducted them. Faith's triumphs differ according to "times and seasons" and circumstances. It is instructive to ponder the specific event cited by the Spirit of God and to view it against the background of the life under review.

Details of Jacob's long eventful life are recorded in the book of Genesis. As the writer of Hebrews surveyed with Spirit-given perception the struggles and triumphs of the "supplanter" who became a "prince with God", why did he choose to recapture for us, in the few words quoted at the head of this page, those memorable scenes at the deathbed of the aged patriarch? Was this the high peak in Jacob's pilgrimage of faith? Whether that be so or not, it was the incident chosen by the Spirit of God to impress upon us that in the school of faith what matters is the end-product. God's servants are expendable. At times in the path of obedient faith there are experiences which may seem a leap in the dark, but God works in ways of His own, and His ways are perfect. Sometimes the pilgrim's way is dark, and the hill is steep. At such times the word from the Lord is: "He that walketh in darkness, and hath no light, let him trust in the name of the Lord, and stay upon his God" (Is.50:10).

From the time of his early encounter with God at Bethel (Gen.28), Jacob had been assured and re-assured by divine promise that he and his family were on the mainline of a great purpose of God. Yet setbacks and calamities were so prevalent in his life that he was frequently at the end of his tether. Possibly, his blackest days were those brought about by the circumstances which wrung from him the despairing verdict, "all these things are against me" (see Gen.42:36-38). How mistaken he was! Soon he would be permitted to learn how wonderfully another Hand had been at work for him.

In spite of its lurid patches and dark clouds, Jacob's life had a radiant sunset. As he stood back and contemplated the scene so graphically depicted in Genesis chapters 48, 49, the writer of Hebrews was captivated by it. We look at it once more. 'By faith Jacob, when he was a dying, blessed each of the sons of Joseph; and worshipped, leaning upon the top of his staff". "I had not thought to see thy face," said the old warrior to Joseph, "and, lo, God hath let me see thy seed also".

Touching moments for father, son and grandsons: history in the making! As Joseph presented the two boys to his father for blessing he positioned them in order of birth: Manasseh, the elder, at his father's right hand. Observing that Jacob crossed his hands, placing his right hand on Ephraim's head; Joseph remonstrated, "Not so, my father: for this is the firstborn…" "I know it, my son, I know it", was the firm reply. The younger would be first.

To the old man, bent with age, natural sight impaired but faith strong, everything was clear now. All had come right in the end! The past was explained and understood; the future was secure and glorious. "And Israel said unto Joseph, Behold I die: but God shall be with you, and bring you again unto the land of your fathers" (Gen. 48:21). And then he worshipped, leaning upon the top of his staff. The lesson?

"God moves in a mysterious way,

His wonders to perform;

He plants His footsteps in the sea,

And rides upon the storm.

Ye fearful saints, fresh courage take;

The clouds ye so much dread

Are big with mercy, and shall break

In blessings on your head.

Judge not the Lord by feeble sense,

But trust Him for His grace;

Behind a frowning providence

He hides a smiling face."

# CHAPTER SEVENTEEN: THE SHIELD OF FAITH (DAVID HYLAND)

IN EPHESIANS CHAPTER 6:1-20 Paul describes the armour which enables the believer to be "a good soldier of Christ Jesus" (2 Tim.2:3). The fourth piece of armour which is available to equip the believer for spiritual conflict is "the shield of faith".

Shields come in various shapes and sizes. The Greeks often used a small circular shield which covered only part of the body. Paul uses the Greek word 'thureos' which describes the large rectangular shield, used by the Romans, which covered the whole body. According to Armitage Robinson this type of shield "consisted ... of two layers of wood glued together and covered first with linen and then with hide: it was bound with iron above and below". They were sometimes saturated in water. Their purpose was to put out darts or arrows which had been dipped in a combustible material such as pitch, set alight and fired.

Believers need to anchor faith in the promises of God to shield themselves from "the fiery darts of the evil one" who tempts into sin. The writer to the Hebrews refers to "sin which clings so closely" (Hebrews 12:1 RSV). if you or I have a "besetting" sin, an area of life where repeated failure has been experienced, the Devil will be aware and exploit it. It seems probable, however, that for the author of Hebrews the "sin which clings so closely" is the sin of unbelief; believers are to "lay aside" this besetting sin. In chapter 11 he calls to mind the exploits of men and women of faith who took God at His Word and lived their lives accordingly.

God "is a shield to those who take refuge in Him" (Prov.30:5 RSV). By faith we realize that in God alone can we find refuge in the day of trouble. When temptation comes, faith lays hold of the power of God. When doubt or depression threaten, faith lays hold of the promises of God. Resolute faith, Paul says, not only stops, but extinguishes Satan's fire-tipped darts.

One advantage of the large doorshield used by the Romans was that several could be placed side-by-side and even one above another. This enabled a group of men to present a united front to the enemy, whose missiles met a wall of resistance. The Devil attacks individuals, but he also attacks the families of believers and churches of God. The serpent attacked Adam through his wife, with disastrous consequences. The Church of God in Smyrna was warned "the Devil is about to throw some of you into prison, that you may be tested" (Rev.2:10 RSV). The only way the Adversary's attacks can be repulsed is for each individual to "put on the whole armour of God" and for all to take shelter behind a protective "shield of faith".

# CHAPTER EIGHTEEN: FAITH AND UNBELIEF (JOHN TERRELL)

UNBELIEF, LET IT BE clearly stated at the outset, is not just something which "happens" to an individual. It is consistently presented in Scripture as an attitude and state of heart which involves the will. The use of the word 'unbelief' in the New Testament Scriptures repeatedly underlines this fact through the context and emphasis, as we shall see. Although indistinguishable in essence from the simple thought of "lack of faith", unbelief is demonstrated in the Word as an evil in itself, not purely as the absence of the virtue of faith. An act of an individual's will is intimately concerned in arriving at a state of unbelief with all the potential this holds for spiritual disaster. This submission we shall seek to illustrate from Scripture as we proceed to think of this menacing adversary as it affects, firstly the sinner, secondly the saint, and thirdly the people of God.

**Unbelief - Its Effects in the Sinner**

Although our primary concern is with the spiritual condition and life of those whose "life is hid with Christ in God", it is in connection with the unsaved person that we get the most vivid picture of the power and peril of unbelief, and the most arresting appreciation of its consequences. It is in fact the very essence of sin: "Whatsoever is not of faith is sin" (Rom.14:23). Perhaps one of the most solemn verses of all Scripture is Revelation 21:8: "But for the fearful, and unbelieving, and abominable, and murderers, and fornicators, and sorcerers, and idolaters, and all liars, their part shall be in the lake that burneth with fire and brimstone; which is the second death".

Prominent in the horrifying list of those who will call forth the divine eternal judgement, are the "unbelieving". Here is the ultimate in tragedy, the lake of fire which is the second death: men and women beyond the reach of the mercy of God. Yet it is just this mercy which human unbelief calls forth from a God of infinite patience and love. It was mercy which Saul of Tarsus received, "... because I did it ignorantly in unbelief" (1 Tim.1:13). It was mercy which a poor epileptic boy's father craved of the Master, "Lord have mercy on my son (Matt.17:15), and which drew the dear man so gently but firmly to the point where he cried out, "I believe, help Thou mine unbelief" (Mk.9.24).

"If Thou canst!" had been the Saviour's challenge, "All things are possible to him that believeth". What a spiritual breakthrough for the man, even apart from the mighty blessing of his boy's health! What a grief to the Lord when in His own country, "He could there do no mighty work, save that He laid His hands upon a few sick folk, and healed them. And He marvelled because of their unbelief" (Mk.6:5,6). In the latter instance we see clearly the element of undisguised rebellion; a wilful decision not to believe; an elective non-acceptance of "the carpenter ...". Such then in stark outline is something of the strength and subtlety of this foe of our faith.

## Unbelief - Its Effects in the Saint

It is hardly to be expected that so formidable an adversary as ours would neglect to employ a weapon against believers which had proved so effective in keeping men from the Saviour. Indeed susceptibility to unbelief in Christian life is both universal and unending. We may well covet the commendation earned by Abraham and recorded in Romans 4:20, "he wavered not through unbelief". Yet each individual's Christian experience bears its own witness to our readiness to be found guilty.

We can learn much from the experience of the disciples as well as from the instruction and warning given to them in the New Testament. The case of the healing of the epileptic boy as recorded in the Synoptic Gospels, offers penetrating lessons. The Lord's disciples had rejoiced in the power conferred on them to heal the sick and cast out demons. One would expect their faith to be greatly strengthened, as well as the Lord's name widely glorified. Yet their failure to deal with the evil spirit afflicting this particular boy drew forth a sharp rebuke from the Lord. To the question-one in which we can almost detect a petulant note – "Why could not we cast it out?" the Master replied, "Because of your little faith" (Matt.17:19,20).

Alongside this, however, must be set the reply recorded in Mark 9.29, "This kind can come out by nothing, save by prayer". The light of faith on the part of the lad's father, breaking through the mists of his confessed unbelief, stands in striking contrast to the lack of faith in the disciples. The fact that the incident occurred immediately following the transfiguration of Christ in the mount carries great significance. Luke tells us that, "He ... went up into the mountain to pray" (Lk.9:28). Had the Lord perceived a deterioration in the prayer-life of His disciples? And was this directly related to a waning faith whose effect on their spiritual powers had left them perplexed and questioning? So it would appear, when we consider the two replies of the Lord as recorded by Matthew and Mark respectively. This would point to the vital importance of unbroken communication with God in undergirding our faith and in keeping at bay our unrelenting enemy - unbelief.

Clearly our opening the door to this foe can be an insidious process, ready to be revealed in circumstances demanding exceptional spiritual strength. Nor was this the only occasion the Lord Jesus had to rebuke His own for their unbelief. It must have tarnished for the disciples the brilliance of that resurrection occasion when Christ had to upbraid them "with their unbelief and hardness of heart". Twice it is recorded in that same chapter that "they ... disbelieved", and again, "neither believed they them" (Mk.16:11,13,14). In the case of Thomas, where the wilfulness of unbelief is demonstrated, if anywhere, the Lord offers to generations of believers yet unborn the exhilarating blessedness of those who "have not seen and yet have believed".

It is, however, solemn to appreciate the context in which the saint of God receives his gravest scriptural caution against the pernicious effects of unbelief. And so we turn to:

**Unbelief - Its Effects on the People of God**

The epistle to the Hebrews chapter 3 is our principal text now, and with it the intimately related precepts of chapter 4. Paul had written to the Romans of the spiritual tragedy which befell Israel. He simultaneously reminded the saints in the church in Rome of the basis of their spiritual position, "by their unbelief they were broken off, and thou standest by thy faith" (Rom.11:20). Now, to the Hebrews, the faithfulness of "the Apostle and High Priest of our confession" is presented, and followed up immediately with a reminder of His glorious role as Son over God's house, and the conditional character of the saints' standing in that house. "Wherefore, even as the Holy Spirit saith, ... Harden not your hearts", and further "Take heed, brethren, lest haply there shall be in any one of you an evil heart of unbelief in falling away from the living God" (Heb.3:1,6,7,12).

Unbelief poses a threat of major proportions to the very existence of a house for and of God on earth, today. Moreover it is unbelief in "any one of you" which is specified. As this malignant disease gains a grip on the hearts of individuals and spreads to others, the entire spiritual fabric of the people of God becomes threatened. The association of "hardness of heart" with unbelief and the direct warning against hardening, again underline the fact that unbelief involves a person's will, and entails no less than a spirit of rebellion.

The direct legacy of Israel's unbelief was a disastrous failure to enter into the promised rest of Jehovah (Heb.3:19). The parallel of the spiritual Israel today is drawn by the Holy Spirit in Hebrews 4, with unerring precision, "There remaineth therefore a sabbath rest for the people of God". Also, in chapter 4 of Hebrews we find, in very close association with unbelief, the sin of disobedience. The words used in the New Testament Greek, and rendered "unbelief" and "disobedience" in the English Bible, stand very closely related. They are the twin evils which infect the heart and pervert the will towards revolt against the word and command of God.

Do Christians gathered out today from sectarian spiritual associations, and into the house of God expressed we submit, in churches of God - appreciate the spiritual "rest of God?" Do we apprehend the utterly relentless pressures which unbelief imposes upon us as the foe of our faith? Do we sometimes feel threatened with despair in contending for the Faith "which was once for all delivered unto the saints" (Jude 3), overshadowed by our own natural propensity towards "an evil heart of unbelief in falling away from the living God?" If so, we may find the answer of encouragement in the words which open Hebrews 3 and in those which close Hebrews 4, words which surround with reassurance the solemnity and warning of these two chapters, "Consider the Apostle and High Priest of our confession, even Jesus", and, "Having then a great High Priest, ... Jesus the Son of God, let us hold fast our confession". Having a Great High Priest who has fully shared our temptations, "let us therefore draw near with boldness unto the throne of grace".

And so we are returned to the lesson which the Master taught His disciples when their faith failed; to the great divine Intercessor who prayed for Peter, when besieged by spiritual foes, "that thy faith fail not"; to the almighty Saviour whose presence and grace alone provide the bulwark against this and all of the foes of our faith.

# CHAPTER NINETEEN: A QUESTION OF FAITH - IS YOUR GOD ABLE? (GUY JARVIE)

NAZARETH, THE PLACE where the people should have known the Lord best, was the place where they knew least about Him. When they heard about the wonderful things which He did in other places they were astonished at Him. They were astonished at Him, and He marvelled at their unbelief. That unbelief tied His hands (if we may so speak), so that there He could do no mighty work (Mk.6:5,6). What an awful thing unbelief is! And what mighty power is available to faith! How careful we should be lest we limit the power of God to our small thoughts or expectations!

Is your God able? What wonderful words are written in Ephesians 3.20! Yes, He is able! As you look out upon your life, there are "some uncertainties and some hopes". Is your God able? If we doubt His power then we may not see it in our lives, though we may hear about it in the lives of others. But faith can grow. Oh thank God for this! We need not always be limited by our little faith which hinders the power of God. Our faith must grow, if we are to see the power of God manifest in our lives. How will our faith grow? By meditation on the word and by prayer. As you consider that verse in Ephesians 3, your faith will become stronger. God is able to do more than we can ask or even think. What a great God we have! There is nothing great about us, but what a great God we have! Take time to think about that verse. If you do, you will begin to mount up with wings like an eagle (Is.40:81).

Another verse which will be a great help to you, you will find in Psalm 18:30. God never errs - never. This is a great help to our faith. We may err - and we do. Our best friends may err - and they do. But our God never errs. His way is perfect. What should we do when we read such verses? Why we should kneel down and thank God for His word, and tell Him that we believe Him. Unbelief of God is the most ridiculous thing in the world. Our reason alone tells us that the God who so perfectly formed the heavens and the earth, and all that is in them, must be perfect in all His ways. But when we read His word, and see that His love is as great as His power, we bow our knees and adore Him, through our Lord Jesus Christ.

What is necessary then, if we are to see His power in our lives? Prayer added to faith! In Nazareth they did not ask for healing because they did not believe in His power, and He marvelled at their unbelief! Sometimes we ask for little, and expect little because of our little faith. We do not know Him sufficiently! This is partly due to a lack of prayer in our lives. If prayer is to become a real thing in our lives (and it must be, if our faith is to grow) then we must take time for prayer. We are often in a hurry, but God never is! Take time! Guard against being in a hurry in prayer ... God can accomplish more in a day than we can in a lifetime!

More than a few minutes of prayer, and a few minutes of Bible reading, are needed, if our faith is to grow. Faith is the great power-bringer. Daniel was great in faith, because he was great in prayer (6:10), and great in meditation on the word (9:2). There are no substitutes in our lives for these! What about our prayer life, our secret times with God? What about our time meditating on the word? "Speak, Lord, for Thy servant heareth," must be our daily prayer, and we must take time to hear Him "speaking." If possible the morning hours are the best. But at all costs, appoint a time and keep to it. No man or woman has ever done great things for God who did not do them by His power. No man or woman has ever had power who was weak in faith and prayer.

Dear disciple, what you accomplish in your life will correspond exactly to your faith and prayer. I repeat again - let us take time for secret prayer, for communion with God, and for meditation on the word. As we do our faith will grow, and as our faith grows go will our peace and joy, and through us the power of God will be made manifest to others.

# CHAPTER TWENTY: DOUBTING THOMAS (KEN DRAIN)

IT IS SAD HOW OFTEN a person is stereotyped because of one act or indiscretion. Thomas Didymus is known to all as 'Doubting Thomas' yet this title may prevent us from seeing him as one who possessed many lovely qualities. Didymus means twin. Surely there can be no closer natural bond than to be a twin. Often identical twins think the same thoughts, feel the same pain, share the same joys and almost act as two persons harmonized into one entity. To be separated may be a traumatic experience. We do not read of Thomas' twin. Did Thomas sacrifice the closeness of this relationship to follow the Lord? Have you been called upon to separate yourself from a relationship which you cherish to follow the Lord? It may not be a brother, sister, or even a friend but rather the close love of your life whatever form that may take.

When he thought the Lord was going to die it was Thomas who said, 'Let us also go, that we may die with Him' (Jn.11:16). What an expression of solidarity. What a commitment to love and unquestioning devotion. The Lord needs men and women of this calibre today - those who are prepared to enter into the fellowship of His sufferings, His rejection, His shame, those who are prepared to go outside the camp' with Him. What a lovely insight into Thomas' character that his love was so strong he was willing to follow to the end and pay the ultimate price. Are you equally committed, is your love so strong that you will follow to the end whatever the cost? "Lord Jesus, 'tis my purpose, To serve Thee to the end."

The Lord knew the weakness which would be exposed in Thomas' faith and still He chose him to be an apostle. Behind that weakness glowed the lovely qualities of love for the Lord and a desire to follow Him.

From his doubt he would be lifted to follow on. Thomas was one of those who saw the Lord ascending into heaven and received the angelic promise of His return. Thomas was also one of those found in the upper chamber, continuing steadfastly in prayer.

After the crucifixion Thomas was so preoccupied with the Lord's death and the disfigurement of Calvary that he could not accept the reality of resurrection - he needed tangible evidence. Jesus wasn't in the company when Thomas expressed his doubts, yet the Saviour knew and understood his difficulties and addressed them. With compassion for his human failing the Lord gave him the opportunity to experience the two things which be bad requested, to put his finger into the nail prints and his band into the spear print It was sufficient just to see the wounds, but did Thomas actually feel them, perhaps to share the revulsion of the dreadful mutilation of his Lord's body? In any case he was fully reassured of the One who stood before him as he said, 'My Lord and my God'.

Today we believe in the nail-pierced, spear-wounded Man of Calvary. We weep at His suffering, we wonder at His sacrifice and we say with dear blind Fanny Crosby: "I shall know Him, by the print of the nails in His hand." To the blind, tactile responses mean so much, but for the re-union with her Saviour there would be no need to feel the nail prints, she will be able to see them, for her eyes will be open to experience that soul thrilling rapture when she views His blessed face. "Blessed are they that have not seen, and yet have believed" (Jn.20:29).

What a privilege it was for those disciples to see, touch and hear the living and risen Saviour, but what a blessing is accorded those who know Him by faith! Have you ever doubted the Lord's hand in your life? Have you ever asked for tangible evidence? So often we echo the cry of that distraught father who said, "I believe; help Thou mine unbelief" (Mk.9:24). Shall we allow our eyes to be drawn from Him, allow our faith to fail so that we turn back from following on? Yes we may have our moments, but may our heartfelt prayer be for faith to continue. The Lord understood Thomas' weakness and He understands ours.

Thomas did not doubt the Lord's word but did not understand it when He said, "And whither I go, ye know the way" (Jn.14:4). It was as a response to the simple question "... how know we the way?" that we gained yet another great classic of Scripture used so much in the preaching of the Gospel: "I am the Way, and the Truth, and the Life: no one cometh unto the Father, but by Me". How often do we not quite understand God's hand in our lives and we are caused to question. Yet in His gracious compassion He listens and responds, and we learn such valuable spiritual lessons. We should never doubt God's will in our lives but we may certainly ask Him to reveal Himself to us.

Doubts in your life may well be a cause for turning from following the Lord. Indeed Satan will use your doubts to make you believe that you are of no value to God, and therefore there is no point in continuing. Let us all learn from Thomas that when Jesus calls us He will carry us through our doubts and encourage us to follow on, to be still found with God's people, to be still found continuing steadfastly in prayer.

"When doubts and fears arise,

Teach me Thy way;

When storms O'erspread the skies,

Teach me Thy way.

Shine through the cloud and rain,

Through sorrow, toil and pain;

Make Thou my pathway plain,

Teach me Thy way."

How easy it is to sing these words when skies are blue and life ahead seems so full of blessing and promise. Yet how many falter when the darker clouds come, when the sky assumes a menacing and oppressive blackness, when we are buffeted by the storm. We become unsettled with misgiving and doubt. We begin to wonder what the future holds, and we feel unable to cope. How many times have we longed for some small but tangible reassurance that God is still with us in our trouble, some practical evidence that things will be all right How often do we pray for the physical rather than the spiritual and expect a physical response. We want to see to believe. "Make haste to answer me, O LORD; my spirit faileth" (Ps.143:7).

How often do we read in God's Word of those who were filled with doubt. It was Peter, that impetuous and dearly loved disciple, who when he was walking on the waters, took his eyes off the Lord and saw the natural responses of the elements, causing him to hear the Lord's admonition "O thou of little faith, wherefore didst thou doubt?' (Matt.14:31). Yet Peter was to follow on and he eventually gave his life for his Saviour.

Doubt would appear to be the result of a lack of faith. The disciples were told "If you have faith, and doubt not it shall be done" (Matt.21:21). Abraham "... wavered not through unbelief, but waxed strong through faith ..." (Rom.4:20). "But he that doubteth is condemned if he eat, because be eateth not of faith" (Rom.14:23). 'But let him ask in faith, nothing doubting for he that doubteth is like the surge of the sea driven by the wind and tossed" (Jas.1:6).

Perhaps the magnitude of our doubt is a measure of our faith and so we need to ask the Lord to strengthen our faith. But we do take courage in that the One who was "in all points tempted, like as we" is also the One who says, "I will in no wise fail thee, neither will I in any wise forsake thee" (Heb.13:5).

# CHAPTER TWENTY-ONE: FAITH IN ACTION – THE WIDOW OF ZAREPHATH (REG DARKE)

THERE WAS NO WIDOW'S pension in the days of Elijah. Nevertheless, the widow of Zarephath received a generous guarantee from God because she made the prophet a meal from her tiny store of food. God undertook to provide her with daily food during famine and drought. The God of heaven, who is Jehovah Jireh, the Lord who provides, has not changed since the days of Elijah, and His promises are just as valid now as they were then. Many of God's people can testify to this.

It is from the Lord Jesus that we learn that there were many widows in Israel during the famine of Elijah's day; but it was to the widow of Zarephath that the prophet was sent (Lk.4:26). Human reasoning would count this strange. No husband, a dependent son; where could she obtain food during such a dearth? Elijah had nothing; the widow had little more. Both trusted in Jehovah Jireh. Elijah's request to the widow appears insignificant. A little water, a morsel of bread. But during a famine and drought this would present problems to a faithless, self-protecting person. The widow had a handful of meal, a little oil, a few sticks of wood. Elijah asked her to make his first, and bring it to him, then to get hers and her son's. This was the challenge to faith. But with it always comes the promise.

Note what Elijah said: "For thus saith the LORD, the God of Israel, The barrel of meal shall not waste, neither shall the cruse of oil fail, until the day that the LORD sendeth rain upon the earth" (1 Kin.17:14). The Master tells us that the heaven was shut up for three and a half years (Lk.4:25). James tells us that Elijah prayed fervently that it might not rain for three and a half years (5:17). Yet the guarantee was given that the barrel of meal and the cruse of oil would not fail until the day the Lord sent rain on the earth. We can only marvel at the faith of Elijah, and the faith of the widow; but we can draw strength for our day from the same God who is so unfailing in His provision. Paul transmits to us his implicit faith with these words, "And my God shall fulfil every need of yours according to His riches in glory in Christ Jesus" (Phil.4:19). Believest thou this? "I believe, help Thou mine unbelief" (Mk.9:23).

# CHAPTER TWENTY-TWO: FAITH AND SCIENCE (LAURIE BURROWS)

IN THIS CHAPTER, A non-scientist approaches a thorny subject in the hope that a discussion on simple lines may help other "laymen". The present day preoccupation with the quality of life has brought science to the fore. In the last half-century or so the standard of living for most people has been enormously enhanced by its aid. Almost every man-made article has been improved by the application of scientific principles. For a great many people it has made hard work a thing of the past. Space is being conquered, our knowledge of the universe, of matter, of life, of everything in nature increases daily. But the exploitation of this knowledge has not been altogether an advantage. It has caused severe environmental problems; pollution of air, water and soil are menacing industrial nations. Worse still, science has provided the means for mass slaughter on an unprecedented scale.

Another entry on the debit side is that God seems more remote now that natural events such as storms and earthquakes are attributed to the universal, principle of "cause and effect" rather than to the will of Deity. That is to say, a given set of circumstances will develop upon fixed lines according to the laws of nature and will always have the same results. But God cannot be left out of the equation because the laws are His laws and He is in overall control. "He is not far from each one of us," said the apostle Paul, "for in Him we live, and move, and have our being" (Acts 17:27,28). He "upholds all things by the word of His power" (Heb.1:3).

**Is Science to Blame?**

Adverse trends following in the wake of technical advances are not caused by science, but by man's innate spirit of rebellion against God. Paul says, "They exchanged the truth of God for a lie, and worshipped and served the creature rather than the Creator" (Rom.1:25). These old-fashioned words are still true today. There is an almost universal attitude which concerns itself exclusively with the material and ignores the spiritual. Men have uncovered many of the secrets of nature but in the main have closed their minds to the all-important secrets of God revealed in the Bible. Science is considered to be all-powerful, the world's hope, the world's salvation; and spiritual things are neglected. But science is merely the means by which men are able to advance towards a hoped-for self-sufficiency; it cannot be blamed when people turn their backs on God. Science can be used for either good or bad ends; the real cause of man's problems is his sinful nature. His greed, arrogance and selfish ambition are the major obstacles to human betterment. Sin is a problem of the spiritual realm which science, in the natural realm, is powerless to deal with.

The answer can only be found in the God of the Bible and in His Son who died for our sins on the cross to make provision for the salvation of all who trust Him.

## Definitions

Not everything that goes under the name of science is beyond criticism. Free thinkers have persuaded many people that the principle of "cause and effect" can explain everything; there is therefore no need for faith in God. Such a philosophy encourages its adherents to reason that the origin of the universe, the earth and the human race can be investigated entirely on the basis of current processes. Furthermore, by proper control of nature, the future can be what man himself makes it.

The spread of this kind of reasoning has given rise to tensions between faith and what is popularly considered to be science. But any dispute there may be is not with true science but with those philosophers who misuse science in an effort to justify their unbelief. This brings us to the recurring problem of definitions. What precisely is science? For the purpose of this chapter it will be convenient if we distinguish between (a) facts demonstrated by observation or calculation and (b) scientific philosophy. The latter is an essential study, but speculation may necessarily enter into it, presenting an opportunity for the unbeliever to put forward unscriptural ideas in the name of science.

**Scientific Observation**

This, in its proper sphere, should present no difficulties for the believer. It is accepted that the majority of scientists are able to pursue their work untrammelled by questionable philosophical arguments. The believing scientist will conduct his research on the understanding that he is investigating God's creation and that natural laws are divinely decreed and upheld from day to day. They are instituted by the Creator for His own glory and for man's benefit. "While the earth remaineth, seedtime and harvest, and cold and heat, and summer and winter, and day and night shall not cease" (Gen.8:22). Matter has always been observed to behave in a certain way and experience teaches us to accept this reliability as a means of predicting, within limits, certain future events in the physical world. To take a simple example, it is easy to arrange in advance the best time for bathing at the seaside because the tide predictions published by the authorities can be relied upon. This predictability is perhaps the most valuable tool possessed by the scientist.

**Miracles**

But the foregoing view of Providence has as its corollary the implication that the supreme God who framed the laws can also vary them by specific ends according to His will. On this basis the Christian should have no difficulty in believing the biblical accounts of miracles. The miracles of the Incarnation and Resurrection of the Lord are at the very heart of our faith and are an unmistakable part of divine revelation in holy Scripture. These and the lesser divine interventions recorded in Scripture, such as the healing of diseases, the raising of the dead, the stilling of the storm can be accepted without offending reason. On the same principle the creation of the universe out of nothing is not unreasonable.

Divine power is never exercised capriciously; God's miraculous interventions are for the benefit of man or for judgement on wrong-doing. They do not destroy the consistent operation of the laws of nature for they are purely local and temporary changes.

**Speculation**

The view that the scientist is investigating God's creation is not accepted by the atheistic philosopher. He mocks the Word of God and thinks that "all things continue as they were from the beginning ..." He will not accept that "the heavens that now are, and the earth, by the same word have been stored up for fire, being reserved against the day of judgement and destruction of ungodly men" (2 Pet.3:3-17). Such people have a great deal of influence on the minds of men today, for their speculations are often prominently reported in the media. A recent instance was the suggestion that life originally reached the earth from outer space or from some heavenly body. This theory has been given an airing because some evolutionists have now abandoned their hypothesis that life began of itself in suitable conditions which are supposed to have existed on earth at some time in the remote past. On the false assumption that direct creation by a Superior Being is out of the question, the idea that life must have arrived here from elsewhere is almost inevitable. The denial of creation leads men along strange paths! The rejection of creation is not based on science; it is a philosophical notion, but sadly it has become the basis of much modern thinking.

**Bible Truths**

A realistic view of the limitations of science will deter the Christian from accepting without question statements about the origin of the universe which are plainly at variance with the Word of God. However confidently such assertions are made and reiterated, believers will recognize the challenge to God's Word in any system of belief (for that is what it is) which denies the following:

1. The universe came into existence out of nothing by the creative act of Deity (Hebrews 11:3).

2. The solar system, and the earth in particular, are part of a grand design in which man is central in the moral sense (Ps.8:3-7).

3. All life on earth was created by God (Jn.1:3).

4. Adam was the first man, the direct creation of God from the dust of the ground, and Eve was taken from his side (Gen.2:7, 21-23).

Any glossing over of the Genesis account of origins in order to accommodate evolutionary ideas is to be resisted. Although there is mention in Genesis of change and development, this is far from descriptive of the widely accepted concept of evolutionary change. It is vital that the story of Adam's creation and fall be kept intact because the divine plan of the redemption of man depends upon it. "The first man Adam became a living soul" (1 Cor.15:45). "Through one man sin entered into the world, and death through sin" (Rom.5:12). "As in

Adam all die, so also in Christ shall all be made alive" (1 Cor.15:22). These scriptures assume the authenticity of the Genesis story and they are essential to the gospel of the grace of God.

If there was no fall then there is no need of a Saviour; man is inherently good; as he progresses upwards in evolutionary ascent he will arrive eventually at a position where he has the universe at his command. In fact "man can manage without God" is a common belief stemming from such unscriptural ideas about origins. Even if it is maintained that the theory of evolution is a useful tool for scientists and is supported by considerable evidence. It does not follow that the Bible student has no alternative but accept it. The Bible is absolute truth, immeasurably superior to anything emanating from the minds of men.

It may be helpful, in conclusion to quote from an article written by C.M. Luxmore (Ph.D.) as long ago as 1892 and reprinted in Needed Truth in 1918 (p.229): 'As to that which is seen, which has present existence, men of science may investigate it and seek to comprehend it ... But science never has reached and never can reach to a knowledge of the beginning; this God has reserved for faith; to sight it is not granted. The sight of man back into past ages has been extended greatly ... so that he is perhaps able to trace the history of this and other worlds into far remote periods; but his sight is limited, and ever must be limited, to that which has happened since the beginning when God created the heavens and the earth.'

# CHAPTER TWENTY-THREE: FAITH IN THE LIVING GOD (REG DARKE)

SOME MODERN THEORISTS tell us that God is dead, while in David's day the foolish sceptic said, "There is no God" (Ps.53.1). The Christian's answer is simply that GOD IS! This is what we are told in Hebrews 11:6, "... for he that cometh to God must believe that He is, and that He is a Rewarder of them that seek after Him". In this wonderful chapter are revealed the twin truths that "FAITH IS ..." (v.1) and that "GOD IS ..." (v.6), and these have been living links between godly souls and the throne of heaven throughout the course of time.

When sorrow, anxiety, and stress come into the life, the believer says, "GOD IS our refuge and strength, a very present help in trouble" (Ps.46.1). The unbeliever says "God is dead", and so he carries his ever-increasing burden of despair through life, as. through a valley of gloom, and he sees no hope, but only hopelessness. Not so the Christian. We have a living God who IS, and who is a Rewarder of them that seek after Him. Abel sought Him with excellent sacrifices; Enoch walked with Him, and was translated to glory by Him; Noah believed Him and built an ark which saved him and his family from the floods of judgement; Abraham obeyed Him, and received a land of promise which his present-day progeny are prepared to defend with their lives. And what shall we say of Jacob who wrestled with Him, of Moses who heard Him from a bush which burned and was not consumed: of Isaiah who saw Him in majestic glory; and of Paul who was delivered by Him from lions, from enemies, and from storms, and who declared confidently "I believe God ...?" (Acts 27:25).

These were men of faith, and had faith's answer to all life's questions and problems. They "wavered not through unbelief, but waxed strong through faith, giving glory to God" (Rom.4.20). They believed that creation was a miracle, that "By the word of the LORD were the heavens made; and all the host of them by the breath of His mouth. He gathered the waters of the sea together as an heap; ... For He spake, and it was done; He commanded and it stood fast" (Ps.33:6,7,9). They believed that God is eternal, and He is the dwelling-place of His people (Deut.33:27). They believed, too, that His Son is eternal, and that, as God, His throne "is for ever and ever" (Heb.1:8). They believed that the Holy Spirit is eternal (Heb.9:14), and that the word of the LORD is right (Ps.33:4).

We believe all these things too, and in an age of scepticism, scorn, and unbelief, we declare our unshakeable faith in the living God, "In Him we live, and move, and have our being", and "He is not far from each one of us" (Acts 17:27,28). He is our great God and Saviour, and through the perfect sacrifice of His Son at Calvary, and the power of His resurrection, death, which men so much fear, has lost its sting. To faith, death is no longer a mystery; and "the unseen" and "the unknown", as men describe the after life, are not in faith's vocabulary. The Lord Jesus has lifted the veil and has shown us that after death there is Paradise or pain (Lk.16:19-31). We know that Christ is now living in heaven because Stephen saw Him there (Acts 7:55), and Saul heard Him speak (Acts 9:4,5).

It is to the place where Christ is that the soul of the believer goes at the time of death, Paul describes this as being, "absent from the body ... at home with the Lord ..." (2 Cor.5:8). We see in these precious truths that the mystery of death has been solved and "the unseen" and "the unknown" are seen and known to faith. The child of God should humbly thank God daily that we know Him through His Son. "And this is life eternal, that they should know Thee the only true God, and Him whom Thou didst send, even Jesus Christ" (Jn.17:3).

God is not dead but living! Sinful man is afraid of God, and has ever been seeking a hiding place from Him. It has been so from the beginning. When Adam transgressed he said, "I was afraid ... and I hid myself" (Gen.3:10). Man is still hiding from God, and today he is using the "trees" of philosophy, unbelief, scepticism, alcoholism, and drugs, because he is afraid. Oh that men would realize that the perfect love of a living God has cast out fear! Christ paid the penalty for sin at Calvary, and God is now able to come to men with the blessed gift of eternal life. God is not dead, but man is! He is dead in trespasses and sins, but a God who lives "willeth that all men should be saved".

Men are being saved. That there is a testimony on this earth for God today, which He calls His spiritual house (1 Pet.2:5), is proof that God is not dead. To us He is EL BETHEL, God of the house of God, and we are His living stones who have been built together that He, the living God, might in very deed dwell among men.

# CHAPTER TWENTY-FOUR: FAITH IN ACTION – EZEKIEL AND HIS WIFE (IAN LITHGOW)

WE READ ABOUT HER IN the book that bears his name (Ezek.24:18). This is the only place in the whole prophecy where she is directly mentioned. The house Ezekiel speaks of in Ezekiel 3:24 and 8:1 was the one they shared together. As far as we know, they did not have any children. She meant much to the prophet of God, who was also a priest (1:3). As a prophet he served God from the age of perhaps 30 (Ezek.1:1) to at least his 52nd year. (See Ezekiel 1:2 regarding the commencing date; 29:17 shows the last recorded date of his prophetic office).

God describes Ezekiel's wife as "the desire of thine eyes". The word desire is translated as lovely (Song of Songs 5:16), "Yea, He is altogether lovely", describing both the moral and physical beauty found in a person. She was the ideal helpmeet and we can picture the home they shared and their deep love for God's things. God was going to test his servant's faith by taking away what was very precious and dear to him, namely, his wife. He was not elderly when this occurred (24:1, where the year is the ninth year of captivity). It is suggested that, in Ezekiel 1:1, the thirtieth year is that of the prophet's age. The prophet states in Ezekiel 1:2 that he had been in captivity 5 years.

By a comparison of these scriptures we conclude that Ezekiel was thirty-four when the word of the Lord came to him - "Son of man, behold, I take away from thee the desire of thine eyes with a stroke: yet neither shalt thou mourn nor weep, neither shall thy tears run down". Many times the word of God had come to him and the Lord's message was faithfully proclaimed, whether of blessing, instruction, or judgement. Never had such a personal word as this been communicated to him. This would touch the innermost parts of his being. Where some may question the working of God, this noble servant said, "So I spake unto the people in the morning; and at even my wife died: and I did in the morning as I was commanded". Here was a test of faith. Ezekiel passed through with full marks and stands beside the other great men and women of faith.

Behind it all was the purpose of God in speaking to His people concerning the desire of their eyes. A far different context this was from the Lord's description of the prophet's desire. The Lord's message is delivered by Ezekiel in 24:21 following their enquiry concerning the death of his wife and its meaning to them. The word to them was, "Thus saith the Lord GOD: Behold, I will profane My sanctuary, the pride of your power, the desire of your eyes, and that which your soul pitieth".

Although they were captives in Babylon, their affection and trust were centred on the city of Jerusalem, believing that they would soon return. Instead of turning to God for forgiveness and strength they trusted in the fortifications of Jerusalem. Now they were going to hear of the destruction that would come upon the city. Ezekiel was a sign to them. As his wife was taken away and he did not mourn for her, so they would be silent when the news came concerning the city. Then they would know that the Lord God alone was their ruler and He alone should be their trust.

God spoke through a faithful man. The cost was great and we are not told of the prophet's sadness, but God knew. He would not allow His servant to pass through what He Himself was not willing to accept. The day came when the One who was all the Father's delight - our Lord Jesus Christ - went to Golgotha's cross and there had all our iniquity laid upon Him. If in our experience we are called to pass through the waters of tribulation or the fire of testing, what will be our reaction? Will it be a complaining spirit, turning back, or the quiet confidence of the Psalmist, "Yea, though I walk through the valley of the shadow of death, I will fear no evil; for Thou art with me". May what was true of faithful Ezekiel characterize us. "At even my wife died: and I did in the morning as I was commanded".

# CHAPTER TWENTY-FIVE: "I BELIEVE GOD" (TOM HYLAND)

THE ABOVE PHRASE IS a concise description of the apostle Paul's testimony during the famous voyage to Rome when he was shipwrecked as recounted in the vivid narrative in Acts 27. At the height of the storm which threatened the lives of the two hundred and seventy-six persons aboard that ill-fated ship, Paul's voice rang out with the confident assertion, "I believe God". The value of a man of faith is always most apparent in a time of crisis. Others may panic but not he. With the calm certainty of faith Paul intimated that although the vessel would be lost all on board would survive. By human standards the apostle's appraisal of the situation seemed foolhardy, yet such was the effect of Paul's message that crew and passengers were transformed. Desperation gave way to hope, and eventually they were all of good cheer (verse 36).

Thank God for men and women of faith who stand for Him when all around seems lost! One such can strengthen the faith of others in a crisis, and turn the course of events. Examples of this abound in Scripture. God needs such men and women today. He needs them in assemblies of God in times of trouble and stress which sometimes occur; men and women who will stand when others fall, who will rally the hearts of the fearful and encourage the fainthearted. Such are above price.

In this crisis Paul not only expressed his utter confidence in his God but also used the occasion to declare his complete devotion to the One in whom he trusted. He did this in the memorable words: "the God whose I am, whom also I serve". We may write this noble confession over the life of this servant of God from his conversion to his final imprisonment and death. "What shall I do, Lord?", the words he spoke lying in the dust on the Damascus road became the dominant feature of his life. Wherever he journeyed, in whatever situation he was found, whether in prison, on a sinking ship or before kings and governors, he always "belonged", he always served.

The apostle's example should act as a spur to us today. In these perilous times we need above all else the confident faith and full committal which were so prominent in Paul's service. He marks the path to effective and constant witness. It is not only necessary that faith be strong but also that devotion be entire, that "I believe" be matched by "I belong". Then the service will flow fully and freely without display or affectation.

# CHAPTER TWENTY-SIX: FAITH IN ACTION – THE FIERY FURNACE (WILLIE STEWART)

WHEN DANIEL AND HIS friends were captives in Babylon, king Nebuchadnezzar set up his golden image and commanded all to fall down and worship it. Daniel's three companions would not fall down and worship the image and so they were brought before the king. When threatened they bravely made answer, "Our God whom we serve is able to deliver us from the burning fiery furnace; and He will deliver us out of thine hand, O king. But if not, be it known unto thee, O king, that we will not serve thy gods, nor worship the golden image which thou hast set up" (Dan.3:17,18).

It is evident that they were not clear as to whether they would be delivered out of the fire or not. The thing they did know was that it would be wrong for them to bow down and worship any other god but Jehovah their God. This lesson we can learn from these men - we must never let what we don't know hinder us from doing what we do know to be the will of God. There is something else we might learn which has been a help to me. Suppose God had allowed them to perish in the flames; would that have meant that their faith was not strong enough? In Hebrews 11 we read of some who through faith escaped the edge of the sword, but we read of others who were slain by the sword. Did those who escaped have a stronger faith or a different kind of faith from those who were slain? No, it was the same faith in essence and strength. Why then did some live and some die? The simple answer is that it was God's will to glorify Himself in the deliverance of the first and glorify Himself in the death of the second.

Sometimes we pray earnestly for a sick friend and he is taken home to be with the Lord. We might chide ourselves and say, "If only my faith had been stronger this would not have happened". May the words "But if not" of Shadrach and his companions be a help to us in the day when our faith seems ready to fail because of seemingly unanswered prayer. God sometimes says "No".

# CHAPTER TWENTY-SEVEN: FAITH AND DIFFICULT QUESTIONS (PETER HICKLING)

ANYONE WHO HAS SMALL children knows that they reach an age, round about five, when every other word is "why?". We don't always find it easy to deal with; sometimes the first answer is quite straightforward, but the next "why?" is more difficult, and the third is impossible.

For example, a child might say "Why does it rain?", and the reply could be "The rain falls out of the clouds". The next question might be "Why does the rain fall down, and how did it get up there?". An adult would then have to explain the mechanism of evaporation, convection and condensation, which he might be expected to know, but the child would probably find difficult to follow because of his limited knowledge. If this was followed by "Why does water evaporate, instead of just getting hotter?", neither parent might know why a change of state takes place at a particular temperature - if anyone does.

All of us sometimes want to ask "Why?". A parent dies, someone suffers in an accident, someone else is unjustly treated, or loses his job; all of them good, kind Christian people, and we want to ask why God should let it happen. Some kindly and well-meaning people will try to console by saying "It's all in God's plan. He never makes a mistake, and He knows best". One doesn't like to pour cold water on what seems a trusting and faithful attitude, but is this really satisfactory? God doesn't plan to do evil things to anyone (Jas.1:13), and the things which are undesirable but not evil are not designed by Him. He knows that they are going to happen, and permits them to happen, but this is not the same as making them happen. The case of Job illustrates this. God pointed him out as "a perfect and an upright man, one that feareth God, and escheweth evil" (Job 1:8). In spite of this, God permitted Satan to touch first his goods and family, then the man himself.

Some of the bad things that happen to us are caused by our own or other people's error, or sometimes by ill will. What would we have God do? To use His power to prevent any act of ill-will or misjudgement by man or demon? If He did this, there would be no such thing as free will or moral responsibility. Every being would be an automaton, doing exactly as it was told. One reason "why", therefore, is that God has restricted Himself by giving man free will - making him "in the image of God" (Gen.1:27). A consequence of this is that bad decisions are sometimes taken, which God could only prevent by a wholesale and full-scale intervention in human affairs which He will one day make. Nonetheless, most Christians would think that there are some occasions on which God overrides human actions, or influences their timing in such a way that ill effects are avoided or reduced. A natural question is "Why doesn't He do this more frequently, or in all cases, to protect His Own?"

One answer is that God is able to bring glory to Himself out of situations where people mean to oppose Him, and to bring good results from evil intentions. For example, Scripture records how Joseph's brothers sold him to the Midianites, and feigned his killing by wild animals (Gen.37). Joseph's reaction was "ye meant evil against me; but God meant it for good, to bring to pass, as it is this day, to save much people alive" (Gen.50:20). Other instances are the way in which Adam's, sin was used as the reason for bringing redemption to the human race, and the way in which the scattering following Saul's persecution was used to spread the gospel (Acts 8:4).

The greatest example of all lies in the death of Christ. The vile betrayal of the Lord was an act for which Judas was fully responsible, but it was part of the chain of events through which the Son of God earned our redemption (Matt.26:24). Scripture shows us again and again that the proof of our faith is "more precious than gold that perisheth though it is proved by fire" (1 Pet.1:7). The originators of the Church of England's Shorter Catechism asked the question "What is the chief end of man?" and answered it "The chief end of man is to glorify God, and to enjoy Him for ever". This is a correct assessment; no greater reason for our existence can be found than that we should exalt God Almighty, who is the epitome of all that is good, and for whose sake everything exists.

Thus God gives to some the opportunity and duty to glorify Him by putting their faith into action; this is an opportunity to be grasped, not a calamity to be bewailed. Is not this sort of test too hard for some? Yes, it is; and God, the all-knowing, says that He "will not suffer you to be tempted above that ye are able; but will with the temptation make also the way of escape" (1 Cor.10:13). To this extent He does use His power to control events and actions, and no one should fear that God will set him an impossible task. If we should find that God has entrusted us with a difficult situation, we can be sure that God will give us the strength to surmount it.

This is the essence of faith. It is a trust in God's goodwill and love; a recognition of the statement of Scripture that "to them that love God, all things work together for good, even to them that are called according to His purpose" (Rom.8:28). Thus the question "why?" will seldom provide much enlightenment, and may well cause energy to be spent on introspection that could better be spent on other things. The past has gone, and we cannot alter it; the future is unknown, except that we can believe God's promises about its general nature; but our duty lies in the present, and God has given us this time in which we can decide to act or not to act. As far as we ourselves are concerned, the simple even rather crude - fact is that we need not ask "why?", just "get on with it".

In the case of calamities happening to others, we are like the child in our initial illustration; it may not be possible for us to have the ultimate reason explained to us, because of our lack of knowledge. Certainly we can say that the view which considers the ultimate evils to be bodily suffering and death is a very temporal and earth-bound one. It is true that while one may adopt the higher spiritual attitude for oneself, it is hard to communicate it to others who have no faith, and see in calamities an obstacle to it. What we can do is to seek to demonstrate it in ourselves, and for that we need the help of God.

# CHAPTER TWENTY-EIGHT: FAITH AND FEELINGS (ANON.)

ONE CAUSE OF UNHAPPINESS to many a young Christian is the changeable state of his feelings. They swing to and fro between elation and despondency. What makes him unhappy is that he looks upon them as a sort of index of the state of his soul, and thinks that there is something wrong with him if he is not in a continuous state of elation. The fact of the matter is that his feelings more often indicate the state of his body, and could he but learn this once and for all it would save him a great deal of honest misery about himself. For instance, how easy it is to be happy and cheery, and to have a heart full of song, on a bright sunny day; and if the following day be raw, dull and rainy, how difficult even to look happy, let alone feel it!

We are very often told to rise above our circumstances, but it is necessary to discern what circumstances are. Feelings are just circumstances and should be treated as such. They come and go, they change from day to day, and we can have little control over them. We can, however, control their effect upon us. We can refuse to allow them to make us unduly miserable. Faith, not feelings, is the ground of tranquillity. Faith grasps the promises of God and brings them home to us, be our feelings what they may.

"Thou shalt keep him in perfect peace whose mind is stayed on Thee" (Is.26:3). The prophet learned this after many trials. We, also, have to learn it through trials. The danger is that we allow feelings to cripple our faith, and we imagine all is wrong when all is well; we look to our feelings to find an answer to our prayers instead of staying our minds on our faithful God. So, also, when we have confessed failure and sin, we shall find an answer in God, not in our feelings.

Cease looking to your feelings, then. They are as changing and fleeting as the clouds of the sky, and they but obscure to us the shining of the face of our beloved Lord, who is the "Yea" and "Amen" to the promises of a faithful God.

"The clouds may come and go,

And storms may sweep our sky,

This blood-sealed friendship changes not,

The cross is ever nigh.

Our love is oft-times low,

Our joy still ebbs and flows,

But peace with Him remains the same,

No change Jehovah knows".

# CHAPTER TWENTY-NINE: FAITH IN ACTION – ELIJAH (EDWIN STANLEY)

LYING IN HOSPITAL, and feeling at my lowest ebb, I knew the Lord was speaking to me. He commanded me to plan for a future that was far different from what I had been doing up to then. It appeared to be impossible - especially considering my current position in that hospital bed! Yet from this unlikely beginning, the course of my life changed, leading me into service for God. God's timing proved to be completely right, and many opportunities for service followed.

My own experience reminds me of what happened to Elijah. He was sent to the Cherith Brook (1), and was presented with a way of life that seemed completely at odds with what he had been doing. He had been a fearless witness for God before the King, yet here he was obeying a command to go into hiding! What sort of service could that be? And he was even expected to rely on birds to feed him - 'unclean' scavenging ravens at that (2)!

Isaiah 55:8 tells us that God's ways and thoughts are totally different from our own, and far nobler. He has the absolute and perfect knowledge to direct His servants and to order the lives of His people, even though the way may seem to be confusing and strange. Elijah knew he was where God wanted him to be, yet the water in the brook was getting lower every day. Had God made a mistake? Had Elijah misinterpreted the command? Should he leave and find a better place? The doubts and fears of our natural minds can so easily make us believe that we are doing what God would expect of us; that we should use our initiative and intelligence; that God surely wants us to be sensible, and not to stay in risky places like this? That may be true when we plan our own course in life and leave God out of things, but when there is a definite command to follow, we are on very dangerous ground to act on our own ideas, however good they may seem to be.

Yet the birds kept coming with food, and Elijah took this extraordinary thing as proof that God had undoubtedly sent him to this place; whatever he may think about it, he must wait for further instructions.

When we are in seemingly unexplainable circumstances it becomes easy for us to question the instructions; to query the purposes of God; even to try to second guess God and take our own course, which we would consider to be far more logical and sensible! Cherith shows us that the instructions, purposes and logic were perfectly ordered, and that Elijah did exactly the right thing by remaining where he was until God said otherwise. Those instructions did not arrive until the Cherith Brook had dried up completely! Elijah shows us that faith - implicit and totally assured faith in an unfailing, all-powerful God - will not be disappointed, but will triumph and will enrich all who trust like this in testing circumstances.

We cannot wriggle out of such obedient faith by arguing that Elijah was different, for Elijah was clearly exactly like us! James 5:17 says that 'Elijah was a man with a nature like ours, and he prayed fervently' Whilst this scripture relates specifically to Elijah's prayer for rain, it does seem to me to be an accurate description of his practice of praying through his difficulties. I cannot imagine that Elijah sat and 'twiddled his thumbs' as he waited for the brook to dry up! I see him fervently praying for his countrymen and their sinful behaviour; for his family and friends in their difficult circumstances, which were a direct result of his request that God should withhold the rain![3] I see him fervently praying for the guidance and help he needed for himself, that he should do what God required and not go his own way.

Faith and fervent prayer go hand in hand. Are we able to echo the words of David in his 25th Psalm - expressing a deep trust in God and the prayer to know His will for our lives, even if we aren't able to understand it? "O my God, in you I trust. Make me to know your ways, O LORD; teach me your paths" (4).

Bible quotations from ESV: (1) 1 Kin.17:1-4 (2) Lev.11:13-19 (3) Jas.5:17 (4) Ps.25:2,4

# CHAPTER THIRTY: FAITH IN ACTION MISCELLANY (VARIOUS)

## ABEL (ROBERT FISHER)

I once heard of a confused lady who lashed out at God for his 'arbitrary' choice of Abel over Cain. She'd been reading the Bible from the beginning and this was an early stumbling-block to her. Later, a friend helped her to find the solution in Hebrews chapter 11... By faith, Abel offered to God a better sacrifice than his older brother Cain (1). In what sense did Abel come 'by faith'? Paul tells us that faith comes from hearing (2). What, then, had Abel heard? Surely we can presume – even from this indication alone – that Abel (and Cain) had heard instruction from their father Adam about the correct way of approach to God.

For surely God had instructed Abel's parents. "The Lord God made garments of skin for Adam and his wife and clothed them" (3). This was the first animal killed as a sacrifice, and to be a covering. Can we doubt that God made the teaching of sacrifice for sins clear at this first opportunity? So Abel came in faith; he offered a better sacrifice than Cain. God respected his gifts, declared him righteous, and so Abel found acceptance. It was not a case of both Abel and Cain each just doing what seemed best or what came naturally to them and then God making some arbitrary choice. Not at all, because Abel came 'by faith'.

This is key, and the reason why Abel's approach to God was reflected in later offerings and the way God ordered his people to bring their sacrifices. God respected Abel's offering for good reason. With such clear guidance, who would dare presume to trust in something other than the blood of the sacrificial Lamb of God – who is Jesus Christ – in order to find acceptance with God? (4)

References: (1) Heb.11:4 (2) Rom.10:17 (3) Gen.3:21 NIV (4) Jn.1:29

## NOAH (BRYAN DOUGAN)

Can you imagine the stares when Noah began to build a giant floating zoo – with nowhere to sail it? But Noah is commended by God for his obedience: "by faith Noah, when warned about things ... in holy fear built an ark" (1). By the time Noah appears in our Bibles, the world was such an evil place that God was sorry He had ever created people! Yet, in contrast, the Bible says that Noah was 'a righteous man, blameless in his time; Noah walked with God" (2).

Without hesitation, Noah responded to God's warning and acted on it. What God asked of him was no easy task. The ark would be 140 metres long, 23 metres wide and 13.5 metres tall; it would take 120 years to complete and Noah wasn't even a carpenter! God provides. He gave Noah a plan and equipped him. Had Noah tried to logically reason through what God was asking, the ark would not have been built. However, through his faith, he not only saved his family, but at the same time condemned the world (1).

When Noah's father named him, he explained his choice, "'this one will give us rest ... from the ground which the LORD has cursed'" (3). When the flood waters finally subsided, Noah built an altar and offered burnt offerings and "the LORD smelled the soothing aroma; and the LORD said to Himself, "I will never again curse the ground on account of man"'(4). Noah had fulfilled his father's expectations.

Christ's work at Calvary gives us rest, but God may ask us to work outside our comfort zone. Will we respond like Noah and be obedient to His call?

Bible references from NASB, unless otherwise stated: (1) Heb.11:7 NIV (2) Gen.6:9 (3) Gen.5:29 (4) Gen.8:21

## ABRAHAM AND ISAAC (BEN JONES)

Picture the situation that Abraham found himself in: God is asking for the son promised to him to be sacrificed. We receive a fascinating insight into Abraham's thoughts through Hebrews 11:17-19, which leads us to realise that it was Abraham's belief that God would raise Isaac from the dead after he was killed.

It is intriguing that such a profound dilemma is dealt with, using Abraham's example, in a mere three verses. Abraham was faced with the choice of obedience to God or protecting his son, longed for and much loved – with the result expressing his faith in God's enduring promises. With this choice, he placed his faith in God's faithfulness, believing in God's supremacy over even death. Abraham placed his faith in a perfect attribute of God. God's faithfulness is absolute and is part of what sets Him apart from us (1). We too have a faithful promise when it comes to sacrifice, in Romans 8:28. We can be sure of our calling, and our love can be expressed through our faithfulness. We can be sure that God will fulfil His promises of blessing, and His purposes through us, and so we can base our faith on His faithfulness.

Bear in mind the contrast between Hebrews 11:19 and the Genesis account; although God's promises were certainly kept, it was not in the way Abraham had expected. It would be foolish to say that we can predict or anticipate God's actions, so our faith must be in the fact that

His ways are higher than ours. His ways will only be clear to us when the fullness of His purpose has been accomplished, thus the need for our faith in His faithfulness.

References: (1) 2 Tim. 2:13

## ISAAC (GUY ELLIOTT)

"By faith Isaac blessed Jacob and Esau in regard to their future" (1). Isaac's clear and definite faith came from a lifetime's experience of knowing God's blessings; particularly when in answer to prayer his wife Rebekah, who was barren, gave birth to twin boys, Esau and Jacob. Isaac demonstrated his faith by blessing his sons, believing all God had promised for the future of his line. In the normal course of events the blessing of the father would go to the firstborn son. In practice, this would mean Esau would be given the double portion of honour, affection and advantage. Esau expected to be given that blessing, especially when Isaac called him and told him he wanted to bless him (2). At this point, Rebekah overheard what was planned and called Jacob to engineer a way for him to receive the blessing.

God, however, was in control and, working contrary to human expectations, overruled to ensure that the blessing of the firstborn should pass from Esau to Jacob, as unwittingly Isaac blessed his younger son. God confirmed His choice of Jacob over Esau, as had been predicted when the Lord spoke to Rebekah in Genesis 25:23, "The older will serve the younger." Why? Because Esau was a godless person (3) who did not value his birthright as the inheritor of God's promises to Abraham.

God used this set of circumstances to achieve His purpose, even though the actions of Isaac, Rebekah and Jacob were not what He desired. So, in what way is Isaac commended for his faith? God didn't condone the actions of those involved, but rather He looked at the sincerity of Isaac's faith and the fact that his faith overcame his unbelief. So Isaac has joined the list of those of whom it is said, "These were all commended for their faith" (4).

Bible references from NIV: (1) Heb.11:20 (2) Gen.27:2-4 (3) Heb.12:16 (4) Heb.11:39

## JOSEPH (LENNIE SHAW)

Joseph was someone who could see the bigger picture ... rejected by his own family, sold as a slave, falsely accused, imprisoned and then forgotten by a man whose dream he had interpreted, he knew God wasn't finished with him. He remembered the God-given dreams for which his brothers hated him. He knew God remembered too and he took God at His word (1). How often do we hear that God's timing is not the same as our own? It took thirteen years of slavery and imprisonment in Egypt before Joseph reached the position for which God was preparing him. Which of us would have had the faith to endure all that he did during that time? He must have clung to those prophetic dreams during his darkest hours when it seemed that he was completely alone and even God had forgotten him. Of course God hadn't forgotten. These times of trial were meant to shape him to become the man who would ultimately occupy the most responsible position in the land.

Christians are not immune from trials and hardship, far from it – God still shapes us.

The day came when Joseph's brothers appeared before him to buy grain for their father's household. How easily he could have taken revenge for their treatment of him. They themselves were still guilt-filled, their thoughts never far from their actions against their own brother so long ago (2). How often had they been haunted by what they had done to Joseph?

As they stood before him, did Joseph's mind go back to his own cries for help from the bottom of the pit as the brothers calmly ignored his distress? He now repaid their evil with mercy, and their betrayal with generosity. He had become the faithful man that God intended.

References: (1) Gen.37:5-10 (2) Gen.42:21-22

## MOSES (IRA WILLIAMSON)

"By faith Moses, when he had grown up, refused to be called the son of Pharaoh's daughter, choosing rather to endure ill-treatment with the people of God" (Heb.11:24-25 NASB). Progressing from a foundation of faith, Moses grew up, refused certain things and chose others. He evaluated the present based on a vision of the future. A life of faith and spiritual growth consists of the things we refuse, and the things we choose.

Growing old is not the same as growing up. I once saw a beautiful bald eagle confined to a bird sanctuary. It was a magnificent looking bird, until it stretched out its wings and revealed a disfigurement caused by malnutrition that made flight impossible. How sad to see something designed for soaring in the heights restricted to hopping in the dust because it didn't 'grow up' properly! Moses refused Egypt's honours. He surely could have had his name for all time recorded in the locked code of Egyptian hieroglyphs, but Moses chose eternal over temporary, incorruptible over corruptible, and spiritual over carnal. He refused to be known as the son of Pharaoh's daughter. Identity is almost as much about what we choose not to be, as it is about what we choose to be.

Moses chose to be mistreated with the people of God. Growing up brings choices. Going with the flow may be easier for a time, but it produces no strength for when difficult choices need to be made. Moses' choice would not have been one 'BIG' decision, but rather a process of learning, making small choices, taking little steps that eventually led him to this place where he felt the unity of his calling with his brothers and sisters by blood above those associated with him by circumstance. For the baby lifted from the Nile, blood was definitely thicker than water. He really was one from among the people of God, and chose to be mistreated along with them. Such a choice could only be made by one who had truly 'grown up.'

With the goal God lays out for us to achieve in Ephesians 4:13, we all have some growing up to do on the basis of our faith. What things are you currently facing which you need to refuse? What choices are yours? Follow Moses' soaring example of looking ahead by faith.

## RAHAB (ANGUS MCILVENNA)

A prostitute! How was it that someone of such ill-repute could be used for the purposes of God? Rahab was not the only one. Years later Jesus said to someone similar, "Your faith has saved you, go in peace" (1). From Joshua 2 we learn the word on the street of Jericho was that God was with His people (2). A sea had been parted and kings destroyed. Morale and courage were low. It was God's will that life was about to change for the inhabitants in Jericho and Rahab knew that.

We don't know the background or circumstances which led to Rahab living the life of a prostitute, but despite this she could, in faith, see God at work: "By faith ... she welcomed the spies" (3). At that point, it was her faith that mattered to God. Rahab showed by welcoming, protecting and helping His representatives, that she could trust that God in heaven would give His reward. Protection was promised to her and to those dear to her.

With faith came courage. The giving of lodging and sending the spies off in a different direction was "considered righteous" (4). She was no longer classified with all those "who were disobedient" (5)/ Brazen Rahab had been used by God to protect the men and to bring about

His purposes. God was at work. The scarlet cord showed that her faith was not a one-off, but ongoing while God's purposes for Jericho were being fully accomplished. Rahab put her faith in God. She acted as one of God's own and asked to be treated in the same way. Her faith was duly rewarded by salvation and a secure home amongst the people of God (6).

Bible references from NIV: (1) Lk.7:50 (2) Josh.2 (3) Heb.11:31 (4) Jas.2:25 (5) Heb.11:31 (6) Josh.6:25; Matt.1:5

## JOSHUA AND THE PEOPLE OF JERICHO (STEPHEN MCCABE)

"By faith the walls of Jericho fell down after they had been encircled for seven days" (1).

This short verse refers to the people of Israel conquering the city of Jericho by God's power (2). Several points are salient after a consideration of these passages. First, the faith that was exhibited was that of the people – collectively expressed. They believed that God would conquer if they followed. Second, and linked inextricably to the act of faith, was the collective obedience of the people – they listened, and they followed the plan through to the fine details. The word of the Lord was given to Joshua, a strong leader, and he passed it on to the people with clarity. Third, the ark was present as they marched round the walls – in fact it was the focal point of the procession. Covered in its blue cloth, it would have been strikingly visible to the people watching from the besieged city. It was not carried by a single individual, but by the group and it contained, for the people, the basis of their covenant with God. They acted in obedience to the commands, in faith. The walls fell.

Similarly, our faith within Churches of God has a collective aspect. It is inextricably linked to obedience – listening to the Word of God, passed on with clarity by strong leaders. We must then, by faith, put that Word into action, down to the fine details. And, crucially, Christ must be present – in fact, the focal point of all we do. His presence among us as the people of God should be strikingly visible to those looking on – in keeping with the type seen in the ark, Christ is still being borne on the shoulders of dedicated disciples for others around to see (3). Collective faith and obedience, together with Christ being upheld as the focal point of our service – this is what will make walls, divisions, barriers and obstacles all tumble down by God's power.

References: (1) Heb.11:30 ESV (2) Josh.6 (3) Ferguson, J.L. 2010, The Parable of the Tabernacle (2nd edition), Hayes Press.

# CHAPTER THIRTY-ONE: YE OF LITTLE FAITH! (REG DARKE)

TIRED, WEARY, DISCOURAGED? Yes, we all get that way at times. So did the disciples as their Master, and our Master too. In the miracle of feeding they saw much grass, much people, but little food (John 6:7-10). A test of faith. "A hundred pennyworth of bread is not sufficient for them" was Philip's observation (Jn.6:7). His eyes were on the hungry crowd, not on the Lord. A mistake we are all liable to make. It is mystifying that after the miracles the disciples had witnessed, they should doubt or question the Lord's ability to do anything. It is questionable whether Nicodemus, the woman at the well, or the nobleman at Cana of Galilee whose sick son was healed, would doubt Him as the Son of God with limitless power, after what He had done for them. How necessary it is for the Christian to know and to understand the mind of Christ. As Paul wrote to the Corinthians, 'But we have the mind of Christ' (1 Cor.2:1.6).

**The mind of Christ**

It is for us too, to know the mind of Christ, a growing experience that enlarges the heart and mind of the Christian. What would have happened to the loaves and fishes the boy supplied, if the Lord had not said, 'Bring them hither to me' (Matt.14:18)? Perhaps it is better for us not to speculate, but rather benefit from the obedience of the disciples in entrusting to the Lord the despised small parcel of food which He used to feed a multitude. Sometimes we look at ourselves, not in humility but in defeatism, wondering how the little we have to offer can be of any use to the Lord at all. Let us balance things out by remembering the value of a single tract to a stranger; a quiet word about the Saviour to a neighbour; the mention of His Name to a relative or friend in a letter; an act of kindness equivalent to five loaves and two fishes given to someone in need. Let us not despise the day of small things, but keep things in perspective. "Little is much if God is in it".

**Our Faith Must Be in Him**

For the miracle to happen to the benefit of the 5,000, the small quantity of bread and fish had to be brought to the Lord. He alone is the dispenser of miracles and blessings. Our faith must be in Him. Beloved brothers and sisters, let us not be discouraged by what we have to offer Him. Bring it willingly, happily, with a loving request that He use it to His praise and glory. Let us remember what He was able to do with a small parcel of food provided by a lad. What a story he would have to tell to his friends! He would treasure the experience for the rest of his days. "What is that in thine hand?" Is it for Him?

## MORE TITLES FROM HAYES PRESS

**If you've enjoyed reading this book, please consider taking a moment to leave a positive review on the site where you downloaded this book.**

You may be interested to know that Hayes Press has many more books for you to enjoy. For example, our Search For Truth series by Brian Johnston now stands at almost 50 titles; each contains excellent reading material in a down-to-earth and conversational style, covering a wide range of topics from Bible character studies, theme studies, book studies, apologetics, prophecy, Christian living and more. Simply search online for "Brian Johnston Search For Truth Series" to locate online stores where the material is available

Hayes Press also has its own imprint with well over one hundred titles available. Our ever-increasing catalogue can be found by searching online for "Hayes Press ebooks". Paperback versions of a number of titles can also be purchased from Hayes Press at www.hayespress.org.

Did you love *Collected Writings On ... Exploring Biblical Faith*? Then you should read *Collected Writings On ... Exploring Biblical Holiness* by Hayes Press!

This book takes a look at one of the most important topics in the Bible and something that God wants all Christians to strive for - holiness. What is holiness? How do we become holy? How do we maintain holiness? What about collective holiness? How are God and Jesus holy?

    CHAPTER ONE: GOD, GLORIOUS IN HOLINESS
    CHAPTER TWO: JESUS, THE HOLY AND RIGHTEOUS ONE
    CHAPTER THREE: BE HOLY, FOR I AM HOLY
    CHAPTER FOUR: HOLINESS AND SEPARATION
    CHAPTER FIVE: THE WORK OF THE HOLY SPIRIT
    CHAPTER SIX: HOLINESS AND LOVE

CHAPTER SEVEN: THE FRUIT OF HOLINESS IN OUR LIVES

CHAPTER EIGHT: HOLINESS BEFITTING GOD'S HOUSE

CHAPTER NINE: HOLINESS AND SANCTIFICATION

CHAPTER TEN: THE SECRET OF HOLY LIVING

CHAPTER ELEVEN: CALLED AS SAINTS

CHAPTER TWELVE: THE HOLINESS OF THE HOLY PLACE

CHAPTER THIRTEEN: WORSHIPPING IN THE BEAUTY OF HOLINESS

CHAPTER FOURTEEN: LIVING UNTO RIGHTEOUSNESS

CHAPTER FIFTEEN: YOUR MOST HOLY FAITH

CHAPTER SIXTEEN: HOLINESS THROUGH PROGRESSIVE SANCTIFICATION

CHAPTER SEVENTEEN: THE HOLY CHARACTER OF GOD'S KINGDOM

CHAPTER EIGHTEEN: THE NAZIRITES' HOLY VOW

CHAPTER NINETEEN: PRACTICAL SANCTIFICATION

# Also by Hayes Press

**Bible Studies**
Bible Studies 1990 - First Samuel
Bible Studies 1991 - The First Letter of Paul to the Corinthians
Bible Studies 1993 - Second Samuel
Bible Studies 1994 - The Establishment and Development of Churches of God
Bible Studies 1995 - The Kings of Judah and Israel from Solomon to Asa
Bible Studies 1992 - The Second Letter of Paul to the Corinthians

**Needed Truth**
Needed Truth 1888
Needed Truth 2001
Needed Truth 2002
Needed Truth 2003
Needed Truth 2004
Needed Truth 2005
Needed Truth 2006
Needed Truth 2007
Needed Truth 2008
Needed Truth 2009
Needed Truth 2010

Needed Truth 2011
Needed Truth 2012
Needed Truth 2015
Needed Truth 1888-1988: A Centenary Review of Major Themes

**Standalone**
The Road Through Calvary: 40 Devotional Readings
Lovers of God's House
Different Discipleship: Jesus' Sermon on the Mount
The House of God: Past, Present and Future
The Kingdom of God
Knowing God: His Names and Nature
Churches of God: Their Biblical Constitution and Functions
Four Books About Jesus
Collected Writings On ... Exploring Biblical Fellowship
Collected Writings On ... Exploring Biblical Hope
Collected Writings On ... The Cross of Christ
Builders for God
Collected Writings On ... Exploring Biblical Faithfulness
Collected Writings On ... Exploring Biblical Joy
Possessing the Land: Spiritual Lessons from Joshua
Collected Writings On ... Exploring Biblical Holiness
Collected Writings On ... Exploring Biblical Faith
Collected Writings On ... Exploring Biblical Love
These Three Remain...Exploring Biblical Faith, Hope and Love
The Teaching and Testimony of the Apostles
Pressure Points - Biblical Advice for 20 of Life's Biggest Challenges
More Than a Saviour: Exploring the Person and Work of Jesus
The Psalms: Volumes 1-4 Boxset
The Faith: Outlines of Scripture Doctrine
Key Doctrines of the Christian Gospel

Is There a Purpose to Life?
Bible Covenants 101
The Hidden Christ - Volume 2: Types and Shadows in Offerings and Sacrifices
The Hidden Christ Volume 1: Types and Shadows in the Old Testament
The Hidden Christ - Volume 3: Types and Shadows in Genesis
Heavenly Meanings - The Parables of Jesus
Fisherman to Follower: The Life and Teaching of Simon Peter
Called to Serve: Lessons from the Levites
Needed Truth 2017 Issue 1
The Breaking of the Bread: Its History, Its Observance, Its Meaning
Spiritual Revivals of the Bible
An Introduction to the Book of Hebrews
The Holy Spirit and the Believer
The Psalms: Volume 1 - Thoughts on Key Themes
The Psalms: Volume 2 - Exploring Key Elements
The Psalms: Volume 3 - Surveying Key Sections
The Psalms: Volume 4 - Savouring Choice Selections
Profiles of the Prophets
The Hidden Christ - Volumes 1-4 Box Set
The Hidden Christ - Volume 4: Types and Shadows in Israel's Tabernacle
Baptism - Its Meaning and Teaching
Conflict and Controversy in the Church of God in Corinth
In the Shadow of Calvary: A Bible Study of John 12-17
Moses: God's Deliverer
Sparkling Facets: Bible Names and Titles of Jesus
A Little Book About Being Christlike
Keys to Church Growth
From Shepherd Boy to Sovereign: The Life of David
Back to Basics: A Guide to Essential Bible Teaching
An Introduction to the Holy Spirit

Israel and the Church in Bible Prophecy
"Growth and Fruit" and Other Writings by John Drain
15 Hot Topics For Today's Christian
Needed Truth Volume 2 1889
Studies on the Return of Christ
Studies on the Resurrection of Christ
Needed Truth Volume 3 1890
The Nations of the Old Testament: Their Relationship with Israel and Bible Prophecy
The Message of the Minor Prophets
Insights from Isaiah
The Bible - Its Inspiration and Authority
Lessons from Ezra and Nehemiah
A Bible Study of God's Names For His People
Moses in One Hour
Abundant Christianity

## About the Publisher

Hayes Press (www.hayespress.org) is a registered charity in the United Kingdom, whose primary mission is to disseminate the Word of God, mainly through literature. It is one of the largest distributors of gospel tracts and leaflets in the United Kingdom, with over 100 titles and hundreds of thousands despatched annually. In addition to paperbacks and eBooks, Hayes Press also publishes Plus Eagles Wings, a fun and educational Bible magazine for children, and Golden Bells, a popular daily Bible reading calendar in wall or desk formats. Also available are over 100 Bibles in many different versions, shapes and sizes, Bible text posters and much more!

www.ingramcontent.com/pod-product-compliance
Lightning Source LLC
Chambersburg PA
CBHW031447040426
42444CB00007B/1005